Information Security: A Practical Guide

Bridging the gap between IT and management

Information Security: A Practical Guide

Bridging the gap between IT and management

TOM MOONEY

IT Governance Publishing

IT Governance Publishing
IT Governance Limited
Unit 3, Clive Court
Bartholomew's Walk
Cambridgeshire Business Park
Ely
Cambridgeshire
CB7 4EA
United Kingdom

www.itgovernance.co.uk

© Tom Mooney 2015

The author has asserted the rights of the author under the Copyright, Designs and Patents Act, 1988, to be identified as the author of this work.

First published in the United Kingdom in 2015
by IT Governance Publishing
ISBN 978-1-84928-740-1

ABOUT THE AUTHOR

Tom Mooney has more than ten years' IT experience working with sensitive information. His current role is as a security risk advisor for the UK Government, where he works with project teams and the wider business to deliver key business systems securely. His key responsibility is to act as an intermediary between management and IT teams to ensure appropriate security controls are put in place. His extensive experience has led him to develop many skills and techniques to converse with people who are not technical or information security experts. Many of these skills and techniques are found in this book.

He has a BSc (Hons) in information and computer security, and is also a CESG certified professional.

ACKNOWLEDGEMENTS

I would like to thank Antonio Velasco, CEO of Sinersys Technologies, Chris Evans, ITSM Specialist and Giuseppe G. Zorzino, CISA CGEIT CRISC, Security Architect for their helpful comments during the review process.

CONTENTS

Contents

INTRODUCTION

When I started my career in information security many years ago the thing that struck me most was the lack of engagement with people who weren't of the information security profession. IT in other departments would shy away from speaking to me as they feared security would stick its nose in and either stop their work or make things more difficult. The business viewed it as a dark art and as long as their security guy said it was okay then that was fine. Most people regarded security as a blocker rather than an enabler. I resolved to change that; I wanted people to see security as an enabler: something that can help you do more business and to create more services. An analogy I like to use when describing security is that of a car: would you get into a car that had no brakes? The answer is no, and so security is like the brakes on your car: you need them to drive. Some people counter that brakes stop you going forwards, to which my response is: do you drive around with your foot on the brake pedal? No, you have brakes to slow you down when you come to a junction, traffic lights or some other hazard. You use them as a control so that you can slow down and assess the situation before proceeding safely. Every driver can see the value in brakes, and this is exactly the viewpoint I want to build for information security. In the information age where everything is connected to the Internet, information security is as important as the brakes on your car: if you don't have it, you're going to have a nasty accident at some point.

I set about creating and building techniques so that I could better work with my peers, increasing their understanding of security. Helping a business understand the risks means it can make more informed decisions and encourage it to grow.

The chapters in this book have been used by myself over a number of years as tools so that I could help my employers build safer systems. Each chapter shares one common focus and that is communication; nothing in this book has been suggested without giving you real value and helping you to better collaborate with your team. I have come across many long-winded documents or overly technical diagrams that are created and then simply filed away to tick a box for some compliance. Each of the things you create from following this book are meant for re-use; they are meant to be changed as the system changes and the risks change. Each chapter is written with examples; the idea is that you read the chapter, understand the technique and then implement it referring to my example if necessary. The book is written in order of how you would follow the techniques described, and each chapter builds upon the previous chapter. The techniques described can be adapted and changed – in fact I encourage it – as I have applied these on many Agile projects and adapted them each time to suit the people I worked with, so you should do the same.

I would like to offer one key piece of advice that is more important than anything else. Make sure you take the time to educate your team on security in a way that they will understand. Make sure you regularly take the time to understand their security concerns and always give them a response ensuring they understand the reasons for your decision. Having your team buy into security and making it part of their day to day work is one of the most valuable information security cultures you can foster; your people will truly become an information security strength.

CHAPTER 1: DAY ONE AS A SECURITY PROFESSIONAL

Chapter Overview

This chapter gives you guidance on bedding yourself into your new role in security. It will help you to get your bearings and explains some of the early tasks you need to carry out to understand your role much better.

The chapter first reinforces the confidentiality, integrity and availability (CIA) mantra, explaining its meaning and how to use it in your role. I then describe the people you should look to meet as soon as possible so that you know what is going on within the organisation and who you will need as allies. The chapter then explores how you can begin to understand the organisation's security culture in order to realise how much influence you have in your role.

Objectives

In this chapter you will learn the following:

- How to build a foundation for communication using CIA
- How to understand the security culture of the organisation
- Building relationships with key personnel
- Identifying the gaps in the organisation's security set up.

Your First Day

Your first day in an information security role can be extremely daunting, especially if you are new to the profession. Often information security is seen as a dark art performed by some elite person, and your peers will have a higher expectation of you and your knowledge of information systems. During a security incident even senior managers will look to you for advice and guidance, so you should be prepared to take on this responsibility and lead when needed.

It is important that you have an overall understanding of the organisation's IT strategy and what systems are being changed and deployed. Remember, in security the attackers only have to win once, whereas you have to win every time. This means there only needs to be one mistake or oversight and a vulnerability could be exploited in your organisation that could have a tremendous impact.

From day one you must get to know the organisation as quickly as possible, its people, its strategy and its culture. You will not be effective in your role until you understand those things.

Confidentiality, Integrity and Availability (CIA)

The CIA mantra is the bread and butter for every information security professional. These three key areas form the foundation of information security. Think of CIA as your weapon when discussing security with IT and business staff alike. Set this foundation for anyone you are going to work with regularly, as it will allow you to develop a mutual understanding. In my experience people pick up the CIA mantra extremely easily.

Confidentiality means that only those who should have access to the data do, and those who do not have a need to access the data cannot. Data is protected from unauthorised access, and this is the traditional view of security.

Integrity means that the data is accurate and that we can rely upon it. Data that is incorrect or suspected of being incorrect has no value as we cannot rely upon it. When discussing integrity ask how much of the data's integrity would need to be compromised before confidence is lost in its entirety, as this will help you gauge how important integrity is.

Availability relates to the information being available to those who are authorised to access it when they need to access it. Information that is not available for use is of no use to us. You may have heard the anecdote of taking the data, putting it in a safe and then dropping that safe to the bottom of the ocean. If that's what we have to do to protect the data then why keep it at all? We can't make any use of the data, and it is a liability not an asset. This is the part people have most difficulty in understanding. Sometimes people think of the data as a physical asset, so for example if the data is stolen, they assume we no longer have access to it. In fact, theft could be a mixture of both availability and confidentiality. It is important to be clear that availability is about whether we can or cannot access the data.

Getting to Know the Business

It is often easy to forget that you and the IT department are there to serve the business; you are a tool and resource to be used for the business to achieve its objectives. This is why it is important to understand the business and what it wants to achieve. In this section I will introduce the different roles and explain their importance.

Senior Managers

When I talk about senior managers in this context I am referring to those who are one level under the Board; typically this will be heads of departments or divisions. Senior managers will often have high-level responsibility in ensuring their department is working to fulfil the organisation's business objectives. The key for you is to ensure information security is on their radar, that when they are overseeing the implementation of their objectives that they consider security. If you don't have buy-in from the top, you will find it difficult to prioritise security within the various IT teams.

Explain to them the CIA mantra so that they understand what each of the three points mean, and it will help if you apply CIA to a specific area. They will then be able to conceptualise security at a high level.

Senior managers are important when trying to change the culture of the organisation and the way it works. Unfortunately people are often resistant to change, but by ensuring senior management buy-in you will have high-level backing to get things done when you encounter resistance.

Business Analysts

Building strong working relationships with business analysts will provide a great insight into the views of the wider organisation. They spend most of their time understanding the business and its needs and then translating this into requirements for IT systems. By understanding their findings you can implement more effective security controls. For example, you implement a new password policy that means passwords now have to be at least 15 characters long. People in the organisation have trouble remembering their passwords so they begin writing them down and attaching them to a sticky note under their keyboards. This security control would actually increase the risk to the organisation of a security breach rather than reduce it. However, as the person responsible for security, people are unlikely to volunteer that they are willingly breaking this rule, so this is where your relationship with business analysts is important. By understanding their work you can better understand the security culture of the organisation and improve it over time, as well as ensuring they factor in security concerns.

Senior Information Risk Owner

The senior information risk owner (SIRO) is a role that you may have not come across before. It is often found in UK government. The SIRO is typically a Board member who has overall responsibility for ensuring effective information security and that it remains a priority on the organisation's agenda. If you are fortunate to work in an organisation that values information security then it may be worth suggesting this role to the Board.

Although the SIRO will champion information security at Board and strategic levels, it is unlikely they will have any in-depth knowledge of information security. Ensure the SIRO understands CIA so that you can develop a common understanding. The SIRO will be key in changing the organisation's security culture as they can raise your concerns at the highest possible level. The SIRO will often come to you with their concerns and rely on you to understand and explain the wider impact on the organisation.

Lawyers

The lawyers or legal team are often forgotten about, but they can be as much of an asset as an enemy. They have great power within an organisation as it is their job to ensure the organisation remains compliant with the law. Ensuring compliance with various laws can be a minefield, hence the need for a legal team. If you are fortunate enough to have a legal team within your organisation, I recommend you meet them as soon as possible. It is useful to build a relationship based on mutual respect: security professionals often have a high-level understanding of the various IT-related laws but it is the lawyers who interpret the law to its fullest. Use the legal team as a resource for advice and also an escalation point when you have legal concerns. As part of this relationship the legal department should ensure it keeps you informed of any proposed new legislation. By having early sight of legal changes you can make sure any security considerations are made early and that the organisation is prepared.

Key IT Personnel

The next step in acclimatising to your new role is to meet the IT staff you will be working with on a more regular basis. Your organisation likely has slightly different roles based on its size, but I would expect the following roles to be covered even if you have people covering several roles.

In this section I will introduce the different roles and their importance. This is also a two-way relationship. If you can build a rapport with these people then they will keep you in the loop with the work going on in the IT department. This is much more important than you think, since when an organisation's security resource is limited you won't be able to be as involved with all aspects of the department as you would like. This can often be troublesome as teams go about their business without considering security and its requirements. By meeting these people and teaching them the CIA mantra you will give them the tools to realise when there is a need for security and encourage them to approach you when you might not have been involved with the work.

Change Management Team

Who

How organisations manage change and deploy IT systems varies widely. Some organisations and small silo teams take care of their changes, whereas others have one overall change-management team with responsibility for all changes. Either way this team or teams have responsibility for determining what and when IT changes and deployments happen.

What they do

Deploying or changing IT systems is rarely a simple task. Who the change affects, what other systems the change will affect, what to do if it all goes horribly wrong and when to implement the change all need to be considered. The change-management team takes the lead on informing the people who the change will affect and if needed provides advice and guidance on the new system. They are also aware of other systems that it affects; for example, if we were upgrading our email system, any IT systems that send email would be affected, not just the users. Also, if we allowed everyone to change systems whenever they wanted, we'd have chaos and probably a broken IT infrastructure. By grouping and scheduling changes we can make small changes to IT systems over time, which also means that if a change breaks a system then we can quickly identify the change and fix it.

Why they are important

The change-management team are the final step in any change-management process. They should keep a record of changes that have been and will be implemented. By understanding their change schedule you can ensure no changes that could introduce weaknesses into IT systems are implemented. I recommend you insist on becoming part of the approval process for changes. By this stage you should be aware of any changes, but this final step will be a catch all for anything that has slipped past.

Network Team

Who

The network team is an obvious one for most people, as this is the team responsible for managing the network. They have a better understanding of the network and the infrastructure it connects than most in the organisation.

What they do

The network team have more responsibility than just the day to day running of the network. They often have the following responsibilities as well: firewall set-up and monitoring, intrusion detection/prevention system (IDS and IPS) and overseeing the efficient running of the network. Monitoring of the IDS and IPS is extremely involved, and because of their understanding of the network the team are best placed to understand the result of this monitoring system. As useful as these systems are, without constant tweaks they flag up a lot of false positives and will not be configured to recognise the latest threats.

Why they are important

Your relationship with the network team will centre around three key areas. Firewall maintenance, in particular rule changes, IDS/IPS changes to ensure they are up to date, and finally any network changes.

When firewalls are installed effort goes into configuring the rules to ensure maximum protection, but over time these rules can be weakened as new systems are implemented. Often the network team are aware of the potential for introducing weaknesses into the network by changing firewall rules, but they may come under pressure from other teams. By forging a strong relationship you can ensure that weaknesses aren't introduced and that more secure solutions are found instead.

IDS and IPS changes will be more of a hands-off role for yourself, as it is likely you will not have the deep technical understanding that the networks team have. Where you can help the networks team is by keeping an eye on trends within security and ensuring they are aware of the latest attacks, as well as which attacks are being most commonly used. This will help the team tweak the IDS/IPS rules and interpret the log records.

Finally we come to network changes. If the network has been implemented correctly, it will be segregated into different security and function zones; this ensures any compromise doesn't affect the entire network but only a small segment. As with the firewall rules this segmentation is well thought out initially but in time segments may become bridged, or even worse segments that should never have any connection have connections introduced. By working with the networks team you can ensure these segments and good network security practice remain in place.

IT Services Team(s)

Who

This team likely has a different name in your organisation. They are responsible for maintaining the different services and systems within your organisation, for example, email, shared drives, office applications and your general desktop infrastructure. Typically these teams focus on getting new systems implemented and working and often security can be an afterthought.

What they do

Their responsibilities vary greatly depending on the organisation. However, they are responsible for the installation, maintenance and general day to day running of the organisation's IT systems. One key aspect of this role is the application of security patches: by keeping systems up to date most known vulnerabilities can be mitigated, and patching is a basic housekeeping task that can have a big effect on how secure an organisation is.

Why they are important

You can assist the team by ensuring security patching remains high on their agenda. I recommend procuring a patch-monitoring service so that you are always aware of the latest security patches for your systems; it is easy to overlook or forget a patch when working in a high-pressure environment. The other way you can assist is by confirming the change-management schedule in time for them to apply security patches.

Finally, when the team is considering implementing a new IT system you need to make sure security requirements are taken into account. This can include whether the new system meets industry best practice, checking historical vulnerabilities found in the system to determine how secure it is, and how much maintenance is likely to be involved in the running of the system. I also recommend all new systems once fully configured and in place undergo a full penetration test.

IT Help Desk Team

Who

The IT help desk or service desk are the first line of support for your IT users. It is their job to log user IT issues as incidents and then provide advice or forward the incident on to the relevant expert. Sometimes this function is outsourced, so getting to know this team on a more personal issue may prove difficult.

What they do

The help desk are the first point of call for IT users and

sometimes customers. They log calls and provide advice where possible, usually trying to fix the caller's issues immediately providing a first-time fix. Where this isn't possible they create a problem record and inform the relevant team. As the help desk is the first line of support, they are aware of any issues first. The help desk should be made aware of any current IT issues so that when they receive calls they can advise and appear to be up to date with the situation. They collate metrics and show patterns in incidents being raised, which is important during a security incident.

Why they are important

As a security professional the help desk is often a bridge between the IT user and customer security incidents and the organisation. For example, if a spam attack is underway using your organisation's email domain, you are unlikely to be aware of it until complaints are logged. Another example is malware spreading through your infrastructure with IT users raising the issue with the help desk. It is important that you remain in the loop with the help desk and are an escalation route for them when a security incident(s) is raised.

You can also be proactive in this area. If you are made aware of a security incident early, you can inform the help desk so they can offer advice to callers. A proactive approach reduces the impact of reputational damage due to a security incident as the organisation appears to be in control of the incident.

Architects/Designers

Who

Architects and designers are responsible for the overall IT strategy of the organisation and provide direction to the organisation. IT architecture is a multidisciplinary function and architects specialise in specific areas such as software, infrastructure and data to name a few.

What they do

Some may argue the difference between architects and designers, but for the purposes of this book I consider them both responsible for the high-level decisions regarding what and how IT systems are implemented and how they should function. They have a long-term view of the organisation's IT strategy and how it will be implemented, and produce the designs for their respective systems.

Why they are important

By influencing the architects early on in the designs you can ensure security is included from the start. Building the architects' understanding of the CIA mantra means they are well placed to ensure security considerations are raised early in the design process. Also, given the architects' technical knowledge they can provide options on how a security issue can be managed; you can help the architect by exploring the benefits of these options and even provide further design options if needed. If you fail to build a good relationship with the architects, you may find that security is often a contentious issue with those responsible for implementing the systems. Security can be quickly seen as a blocker rather than an enabler, which becomes a real issue when people exclude you from design discussions as they believe you will block their decisions rather than help them develop their design.

Software Development Team

Who

The software development team code and develop IT systems, which includes websites and databases. They are among the most technical staff and have some of the deepest understanding of systems. Unfortunately this introverted view often means they fail to consider other issues and systems.

What they do

The software development team is responsible for the low-level design and creation of software code. They work to specific development methodologies; two of the most common being Rational Unified Process (RUP) and Agile. RUP works by developing over a number of predefined cycles planning in changes in an iterative process. Agile is more user centric and focuses on their needs, delivering functionality that can be demonstrated in each user cycle.

Why they are important

A good relationship ensures newly developed systems are secure and that existing systems are maintained.

As we mentioned with the architects it is important that security is included from the start rather than added at the end. Often the software development team focuses on writing code that works rather than the security of that code. Introducing secure coding standards can reduce the number of vulnerabilities and weaknesses in your software. However, sometimes it can be difficult to demonstrate the value of secure coding. I recommend introducing Open Web Application Security Project (OWASP), in particular the OWASP top ten vulnerabilities found in web applications. OWASP explains how these vulnerabilities work and provides guidance on how they can be fixed. The more technical the person, the better it is to demonstrate what you are trying to explain. Showing the developers how some of these vulnerabilities can be exploited will engage them as they will have an appreciation for how the exploits work.

Maintaining systems, especially legacy systems, can be difficult as often they are not as well documented as they ought to be. The software developers have the best understanding of these systems as they were probably the ones who developed them. It can save time knowing who built a system and therefore who can answer your question. This is important if potential security issues are raised and your in-house developed software needs to be patched and fixed.

Incident Management Team

Who

The incident management team manage and coordinate any IT incidents that require immediate action. An example could be the loss of the organisation's email system as the impact is likely to be widespread and great for the business. It is also likely the business will put great pressure on IT to get the issues resolved. It is unlikely you will have a dedicated incident management team (unless IT incidents are commonplace...); instead the team will be brought together and made up of a multidisciplinary group from within the organisation. As a security professional you should be part of this group.

What they do

The incident management team convenes whenever there is a major IT incident that requires management. They typically manage the incident from discovery through to resolution and often look at lessons learned afterwards. They ensure the right people are involved and decide what needs to be done to fix the issue and then coordinate the fix. They also provide constant updates to the business to assure them the incident is being managed properly, and part of this includes an estimated fix time.

Why they are important

It is important that security is represented at incident management meetings, at least initially. The incident may not first appear to be a security issue but until this is confirmed you should be involved. If you have a security risk log, it is important during the management of the incident that you see if the security incident was a potential risk that was previously raised. If it was then the incident could be used as motivation to implement a long-term fix. If the incident was unexpected then the organisation may need to revise its threat landscape and consider the security risks to it.

What is the Security Culture?

Now that you have met the key players from the business and IT, you should have a feeling for the security culture. To help you decide what the culture is like I have noted three key areas that you should consider:

Priority – What is the organisation's priority when considering security? Is it something they think about at the start or do they assess security at the end? When you had your discussions with the business what was their balance of security vs business opportunity? If security has a higher priority then your job should be straightforward. However, if the organisation puts business opportunity first then you must make a strong argument for any security controls you wish to implement. You also need to be careful that you don't come across as someone who is trying to stifle the business through excessive control; remember you are there to facilitate business opportunity.

Attitude – When you were meeting the organisation staff members, what was their attitude? Did they give you plenty of time and listen to what you had to say or were your meetings rushed? I have had people fail to attend arranged meetings, which defines their attitude towards security. Understanding their attitude means you know what level of engagement you are likely to get. When engaging with those who have a poor attitude towards security you may need to ensure you have senior management backing, which should encourage them to be more receptive.

Power – How much power does the security team have? Can the security team veto deployment of new systems if they believe the risks are too high? Does the security team have such little influence that they could shout as loudly as they wanted and no one would listen? If it's the latter then you really have your work cut out. You will probably need to find other ways to reinforce your proposals and arguments. If this doesn't help then perhaps your services will be best used elsewhere...

Identifying the Gaps in Security

Now that we have spent time getting to know the organisation and understanding the culture we need to understand any gaps in security. As you should know, security isn't just about perimeter firewalls but also about process and management. In this section I discuss some of the best ways to understand the gaps in security and how to address them, assuming the organisation has the appetite to do so.

What accreditations does the organisation have?

The fastest way to identify gaps in security is to look at any accreditations the organisation might have. Typically accreditations have a scope. What does this scope include? Is the scope organisation wide or does it cover a standalone server hidden in a room somewhere? Many accreditations are regularly audited by an independent organisation, so read the audit reports and understand the findings. Often an organisation will do its utmost to paint a glossy picture of how it complies with an accreditation; if the auditor identifies any areas of concern, these areas should be of concern to you.

Even if an audit for an accreditation isn't due, it may be worth employing a consultant to carry out a pre-accreditation assessment. Explain that your accreditation isn't at risk of being lost based on the assessment and that you are using it to find areas of weakness. Encourage those involved to be open and honest and that it is much better to identify issues now rather than later.

What is the business appetite for accreditations?

The appetite for accreditation varies from organisation to organisation. Broadly speaking it fits into three categories.

No appetite – The organisation sees little to no value in achieving an accreditation. This can be the most frustrating stance as often achieving accreditation not only proves the organisation is working effectively but can also raise morale as the good work of staff is acknowledged and is meeting a baseline standard.

Appetite for the badge only – The organisation wants the badge that comes with the accreditation but doesn't actually see the value of working to the standard the accreditation defines. A good example of this is ISO27001, which defines the need for various polices. An organisation taking this stance has the required policies but the quality of those policies is questionable; in essence the policy exists to tick a box rather than promote good working practice.

There is appetite for the accreditation as the business see the value and understand the advantages that the accreditation can offer. If the organisation believes itself to follow industry best practices then often it will want these to be recognised as this can prove the quality of service they offer. If your business operates in a particularly competitive market then this could provide an edge over competitors. The other benefit to this is that where an assessment to achieve an accreditation is undertaken any gaps it identifies are likely to be resolved so that the organisation is successful in its assessment.

CHAPTER 2: BUSINESS IMPACT OF BREACHES

Chapter Overview

One of the key issues when joining an organisation is understanding the value of the data the organisation has. As you speak to different members of the business they will insist that nothing is more important than their data. This is of course not true in all cases, and the real challenge is to prioritise the importance of all the information so you know where you need to focus your efforts and time.

The best way to understand the value of data is to assess the impact on the business should that data be compromised. Impact on the business comes in many forms: reputational, financial or even legal; any of these could put an organisation out of business.

This chapter discusses the different types of data and gives you the ability to assess the impact on the business should the data be compromised. I have used broad terms to cover as many different types of data as possible, and the one size fits all method should be applied with some common sense. It is often best to discuss these areas with those who are responsible for the data as they have the best understanding of the impact.

Objectives

In this chapter you will learn the following:

- Broad types of data
- Impact of compromise.

The impact of compromise forms the basis for my quick and dirty risk assessment discussed later in the book.

How to Assess the Impact

In the following sections you will be presented with some broad data types, this is to broadly categorise the data your organisation has and to begin to understand its importance in the wider organisational context. You will then be given some business impact areas in order to assess the impact of the data. What you must do for the dataset you are assessing the impact of is assess whether confidentiality, integrity or availability is compromised. An impact on any aspect of CIA has varying levels depending on the data and the business. For example, customer data will have a bigger impact if its confidentiality or integrity is compromised, whereas compromise of its availability will be an annoyance, but is less likely to impact us as much.

During your assessment you should consider the impact of a single record from the dataset against the entire dataset. For example, if an eCommerce site lost a single product from its online store then the impact would be much less than the loss of its entire product range. It may also help to consider how the impact would scale as a larger proportion of the dataset is compromised.

Finally, consider any links to other datasets. When data is linked with other datasets it can have a major impact on the business. For example, a simple dataset of UK postcodes that is used on the eCommerce website would be an annoyance if it was corrupted. But, if that dataset is used for delivery addresses for our customers then the impact could be wide-reaching and severely damage our finances and reputation.

Data Types

Core business data

Core business data will almost certainly be considered the most important by the business; it should be the organisation's reason for being. This data forms the heart of the business or allows the business to function. For example, Netflix has a vast array of TV shows and films, and if this was lost then their service would be severely disrupted. Another example is if all the products for sale on eBay's website were deleted from its databases then they would not be able to carry out their primary business function. It is important to understand what data the business has and what data is considered key to business function.

Personal data

Personal data is data that relates to people, whether it is your customers or own staff. This is data that relates to their identity, so their name, address, data of birth and so on. Usually this data is kept to facilitate core business function and may be as equally as important to the business. If we borrow our previous Netflix example but this time our customer data is compromised, our business could be impacted in the same way. Customers may not be able to access the service or if the data is stolen, Netflix could find itself on the wrong side of legal action.

Personal financial data

Personal financial data is any financial data relating to customers or staff members. In the case of our staff this could be part of a payroll system so could include bank account details. In the case of customers this could be card and payment details as well as bank account details. This is the sort of data targeted by hackers as it is often a quick win for them financially.

Company financial data

Company financial data can fall into two categories: data relating directly to finance – so accounts, bank cards and other directly related financial data – and data relating to sales and purchases, such as accounting data a company keeps for its balance sheet. The sensitivity of this data can vary depending on who the organisation is and what it does. For example, a government department is required to disclose its financial data each year, whereas a private company does not have to do so. Also, the sensitivity can be dependent on how healthy the organisation's account data is; an organisation in bad financial shape may want to keep this fact from the wider public so as not to scare away potential investors.

Third-party data

Third-party data is another set of data that is hard to define generally, as it is any data given to you by another organisation. It could be purchased or provided under contract. The data could have varying degrees of sensitivity depending on what it is and how the organisation intends on using it. Any controls or responsibilities are defined in a contract between your organisation and the provider of the data.

Impacts

Under each area of impact I have given three levels of

impact, ranging from minor to major. I have purposely included three for each, as these three levels are used later in the quick and dirty risk assessment chapter. The three areas roughly relate to low, medium and high.

Reputational Damage

Reputational damage is often the most difficult to define, as it's hard to put a number on the level of reputational damage. The best way is to think about who would care if there was a data breach. The more people who care, the wider the impact is likely to be, and this impact will also be affected by the size of the organisation and its current reputation. An organisation with a bad reputation is likely to attract extra attention.

National news

Would the breach make national news if it was public? Would the breach be front-page news or be covered by several national newspapers and news channels?

Local or specialist news

Would the breach make local or specialist news if it was made public? Would the breach be published in local newspapers and be broadcast on local news broadcasts? Is the breach likely to only attract specialist news outlets with an interest in the subject or sector your organisation operates in?

Minor discussion

Has the breach only generated minor discussion, perhaps

between customers or those affected by the breach? Have mainstream news outlets shown no interest in the breach? Has your organisation even been approached to make an official statement?

Personal Impact

Personal impact is perhaps the most damaging to an organisation, because it often affects the customers themselves. If enough people vote with their feet and take their business elsewhere, this can cripple an organisation. This type of impact can inflate quickly by the number of people who are a victim of the breach. A recent high-profile breach of this nature was to Sony's PSN network where a number of user details were stolen. The impact of this type of breach varies considerably depending on the nature of the breach and the local attitudes to information security.

Personal finance

Financial data relating to a person can be the most crippling to that person if lost. For example, if an organisation was to lose a person's bank details then there is the possibility of their accounts being emptied. Financial data is often the most sensitive to the individual and can have a dramatic impact on that person's standard of living. It is highly likely that this type of breach would result in both a criminal action against the organisation and a civil prosecution along with the likelihood of being sued.

Personal identity lost

Although still a sensitive area, often people's attitude

towards their identity is somewhat more relaxed than that of their financial information. An example is the amount of personal information people share on Facebook without hesitation. That said, if a breach of your organisation's personal data leads to identity theft of your customers then it is likely your organisation will be held liable.

Minor personal data lost

Minor personal data is any data that wouldn't result in the loss of a person's identity. So, for example, a username and password or even an email address. The breach would still be an annoyance to those involved but it is unlikely to cause long-term distress to the individual. Often the real impact is to the organisation that has to work to encourage users to change passwords so that further compromise doesn't arise.

Contractual Impact

Contractual impact relates to any business contracts your organisation may have with another, either for the provision of a service or data. So, for example, you may have outsourced your cleaning services to a third party or you may purchase Google Earth data. This section details the impact on a contract should the data be compromised, for example if your organisation lost the personal details of the cleaners currently deployed to an office.

Loss of contract

This is a straightforward impact to assess: would the data breach result in the termination or loss of a contract? This impact obviously scales depending on the size of the contract and its importance to the business. But there is more than one way to lose a contract, for example the breach means a clause within the contract itself has been breached causing termination, or you are currently in the bidding process and the breach causes the proposal to be withdrawn.

Contractual fines

This is less severe than the loss of a contract, but again we need to be pragmatic about how it is defined. Some larger contracts may attract larger fines than the entirety of a smaller contract. An example could be the provider of your desktop infrastructure vs the company that delivers the coffee.

Contractual warning

The breach is acknowledged by the third party but no specific action is taken, the incident is logged and your organisation is reminded about its contractual obligations. Although this isn't a severe impact, if a number of these low-impact events occurred then it could result in a fine or termination of contract.

Financial Impact

This is the most traditional way to measure impact on the business – the estimated cost of the impact. Often when the cost of a data breach is quoted people often dismiss it as being inflated, but I want to clarify where the additional cost comes from so that your own assessment takes this into account. Let's say, for example, our organisation is an e-commerce business and on average we make £10,000 an hour from our website; our website is down for six hours so that totals £60,000. The actual cost of the breach will be much greater as we need to add: the cost of the staff involved in managing the incident, the cost of investigating why the incident occurred and finally any actions taken to safeguard against the incident in future. The cost of specialist skills to carry out an investigation can be expensive, as can the cost of new IT infrastructure to prevent a further occurrence of the incident. This is why the figures quoted for financial impact are typically higher than just the money lost through lost trade. The following levels of impact are easily defined; however, depending on the size of your organisation you may need to adjust them so that the costs reflect accurately the impact your organisation would feel.

More than £1 million

The total cost of the incident is in excess of £1 million, which includes loss of trade and the inclusion of incident management and any future actions.

More than £250k but less than £1 million

The total cost of the incident is in excess of £250,000 but less than £1 million, which includes loss of trade and the inclusion of incident management and any future actions.

Up to £250k

The total cost of the incident is less than £250,000, which includes loss of trade and the inclusion of incident management and any future actions. Note that the very fact your organisation cares enough to respond to the incident means that this level is reached.

Legal Impacts

The legal impacts purposely only have two levels, which is because (and I know it's never a simple matter) you are either within breach of the law or not. In the UK we have two types of law: criminal and civil. Criminal law relates to crime and breaches of the various UK laws, and civil law focuses on disputes between two parties. The biggest difference between the two in terms of punishment is that breach of criminal law can result in a prison term, whereas breach of a civil law is only punishable by financial penalty. Often if you are in breach of criminal law you will also invite a case under civil law, especially if the victim feels they should receive compensation.

Criminal law case

The breach has brought about a criminal investigation or the police are considering it. The organisation has liability if such a case is brought forth and will be required to defend itself in a court of law.

Civil law case

The breach has brought about one or more civil cases against the organisation. You will need to consider the size of these civil cases to determine the level of impact. It is worth relating the cost to the financial impact section in order to better assess the level of impact.

CHAPTER 3: BUSINESS RISK APPETITE

Chapter Overview

The business' risk appetite is perhaps the most important thing to know when working to secure a system. When I began my career in security I understood how to secure a system; I had a wealth of knowledge, tools and techniques for protecting different systems. What I did not understand at that stage, however, was how do I know which controls to implement and how secure should each system be. What I did not understand was the risk appetite, which is (defined by ISO31000) how much risk is the business willing to accept in trying to achieve its goals. Of course it's not simply a case of saying I'm this hungry for risk; we need to understand how to define that hunger and then apply it. Risk appetite allows us to look at our list of risks and then decide which risks we want to fix and which ones we are willing to accept and live with.

I recommend completing a risk appetite assessment for the organisation as a whole, as this will help you further understand the organisation's security culture. An organisation may have a strong security culture where they understand the risks but their attitude may be to live with those risks in order to give them business agility and not be tied down by additional security controls. This attitude is fine as long as the risks are identified, fully understood and the impact fully considered. You should then conduct a separate risk appetite assessment for each system you work on using your organisation's appetite as a baseline. The reason for this is that the person you are speaking to may not be fully aware of the organisation's attitude to risk so you can help guide them using previous assessments if needed; but remember, it is ultimately up to the business.

In summary, this is just good risk management.

In this chapter I introduce risk appetite and show how you can assess and define a level of appetite by speaking to various people within the organisation. Ultimately the risk appetite is defined by a manager and those senior staff members who are responsible for the security of IT systems.

Objectives

In this chapter you will learn the following:

- The five levels of risk appetite
- How to describe the five levels of appetite and what they mean
- Risk treatments and how they are applied as security controls.

Risk Appetite

There are five basic levels to risk appetite, which range from averse to all risk all the way to hungry and willing to accept any risk as long as there is business benefit. The appetite level usually relates to the sensitivity of the data it relates to. For example, an organisation that is building a system that relates to people's health and safety is likely to be more risk adverse, whereas a company that is trying to react to a market trend quickly may be more open to risk if the financial rewards are great.

While conducting your assessment it is worth referring back to the previous section and reminding yourself and the person you are in discussion with of the business impact. If the impacts are likely to be severe then ultimately we are going to want to be more cautious in our attitude to risk.

Averse

Every effort should be made to avoid risk, you will always favour the safer option when managing a risk, and if there is no safe option then there is a strong possibility that the system will not be implemented.

Minimal

The organisation still favours the avoidance of risk and will always choose the safest option. However, it is unlikely to go to such extremes as cancelling projects in order to avoid risk. It is, however, likely to spend more time rethinking its plans to mitigate after risks are found.

Cautious

The organisation has a pragmatic view of risk; it understands that with any potential business gain there will always be risks. The organisation will look to favour the safe option unless that option is too costly or technically difficult to achieve.

Open

The organisation is open to risk. It will mitigate risks when the option is cheap and easy, else it will favour the option that provides the most business benefit. However, the business still wants to maintain a handle on what the risks are and to what level they are.

Hungry

The organisation is eager to implement its new system and delivery of that system is its highest priority. It wants to be aware of risks but any mitigations proposed will also have to offer the highest business benefit for it to be considered.

Risk Treatments

Once we understand the business' appetite for risk we can look at mitigations. Typically mitigations fall into one of the following four categories: avoidance, reduction, sharing and acceptance. Your risk appetite helps you decide which type of mitigation should be used. For example, a risk-averse organisation is unlikely to accept retention of a risk, whereas an open organisation is unlikely to favour avoidance if there are business benefits.

The order of the categories starts with the most risk-averse option, with their openness to risk increasing as you go down the list. This enables us to pick the most appropriate control: if a risk cannot be avoided then it should be reduced, if it cannot be reduced then it should be transferred, and if it cannot be transferred then we accept it.

Avoidance

The mitigation for the risk is to avoid it. At one extreme this could be to cancel the project in its entirety or simply build the system in a different way. When deciding to avoid the risk it is first important to understand what the impact of the risk is; for example, would you be in breach of the law. It is unlikely that even an open organisation is keen on breaking the law in order to achieve its goals.

Avoidance can also mean that a risk is fully managed so that it no longer exists, therefore it has been avoided. For example, if a system is likely to be attacked from the Internet then the best way to avoid this is not to connect it to the Internet, therefore the risk is fully managed.

Reduction

This is the most common action taken when managing risk. The reality is that most risks cannot be fully mitigated with controls and that some residual risk will always remain. If, for example, our system has the risk of being infected by malware, we may choose to install an anti-malware system in order to combat infections. We also know that anti-malware systems are not perfect and if exposed to new malware then it may not have been updated to detect the new infection. We must take time to understand how much we have reduced the risk and is this reduction adequate for the project. In fact we have possibly created another smaller risk of the malware failing to detect an infection, which may lead us to consider other controls such as limiting data into the system or even storing incoming data in a fashion that stops it from running. If we go down this route then we are actually applying many controls to the one risk in order to further reduce it. You will have no doubt come across this before, having heard of the term 'defence in depth', the idea being that if one control fails then there are others that will hopefully be able to resist the attack. It's like a castle that has a wall, a moat and men to defend it.

Transfer

Typically the organisation is not able to or is unwilling to reduce or avoid the risk so it chooses to transfer it to someone else. There are many ways to transfer risk: via insurance, outsourcing or contractually. Say our system is going to handle lots of personal data and a breach may result in your organisation being sued; you may choose to take out liability insurance in order to mitigate the claim.

If the system you are proposing to build carries many risks and you believe you don't have the skill or appetite to implement it, you may choose to outsource the function. A common example of this is online card payments where organisations are required to abide by the Payment Card Industry Data Security Standard (the PCI DSS). The organisation may decide that compliance is too expensive or onerous and choose to use a third party, for example PayPal or Sage Pay.

Finally we come to a contractual transfer. Returning to our anti-malware control, it is possible that we may get agreement from the supplier that they will accept a limited amount of liability should their software fail and damage is caused to our system. These types of agreed liabilities are more common when discussing the availability of a system where typically a service-level agreement will be made on how much uptime is expected of the system.

Accept

The final type of control is to simply accept and log the risk. However, an organisation may choose to put aside a cash reserve should it be sued or be subject to any fines for a data breach. An organisation should have a good reason to just accept the risk, as many countries now have data protection laws that must be followed if working with personal data. However, if you aren't working with personal data then accepting the risks may be the most practical option.

CHAPTER 4: THREATS

Chapter Overview

This chapter discusses the potential threats to your organisation, and describes the threats as people with motivations and their capabilities. When conversing with the business it is difficult to describe the threats and risks to a system using technical language. I was giving a presentation on the importance of website security to a business when I was asked, "Why would anyone ever want to attack our system?" I realised at that moment that although they understood the concept of website security I had failed to convince them of the need for it. By using the following technique of creating threat actors you can better convince non-technical people of the need for security as well as build an overall threat landscape for your organisation.

Keep a log of how the threats might compromise your system. This helps you to understand how your system is likely to be attacked and focus on where the most security controls are needed. If you find that most threats would try and compromise the system physically then you can implement more physical controls; if most would attack the network over the Internet then you can ensure you have better network perimeter controls.

Another benefit of keeping a list of threats in this manner is that it allows you to apply those threats to the real world. So, for example, if the police report increased activity by burglars in your area, you can adapt your threats log and take action if necessary. Or, if you read that hackers are increasingly targeting organisations similar to your own, you can work with the networks team to ensure they are extra vigilant. The threat actor model gives you a common understanding to converse and understand changes in the threat landscape. Additionally, if you share your threat log with members of the business, they can also apply their knowledge and understand when a threat increases or decreases. The more people who understand the threats, the more effective your organisation will be at combating them.

Objectives

In this chapter you will learn the following:

- How to understand the threat landscape for your organisation
- How to describe threats in a tangible way
- Understanding the capabilities of threats
- Understanding the motivations of the threats to your organisation.

Types of Threats

The following are the typical threats faced by an organisation. They are generalisations but if you spend time with someone who understands your organisation, you can adapt them for your own purposes. Also take the time to understand previous breaches that have occurred and build threat actors based on those, as this will help you better understand the capabilities and motivations of those who wish to compromise your organisation.

Hackers

When we think about information security, hackers are the

most obvious threat and typically the threat we are most familiar with. Hackers attack our IT system over a network, typically the Internet, and they are skilled and are able to tailor their attacks. These hackers are more than the typical script kiddies and can exploit more than the typical basic security vulnerabilities.

Hackers try to accomplish one or more of the following:

- Financial gain: the theft of financial information or personal information that they can sell
- Control of computer systems to further support other hacking activities
- To show off their skills.

Hackers usually work alone or in small groups, and use bespoke skills. They usually target systems that they are confident of breaching, so they favour easy systems to compromise. They target several systems then focus on those systems that are most likely to succumb to their attack.

Malware Writers

I have purposely separated malware writers (or malware itself) from the standard network attacks. This is because this threat targets different systems and the controls to mitigate this threat are very different. By malware writers I mean the actual malware itself. In recent years malware has transformed from a damaging annoyance to something more dangerous. Often, modern malware will attempt to seek out and steal information, or hold information hostage and demand a ransom to release it. Malware writers favour spreading their software over the Internet when targets visit compromised websites.

Malware writers typically have the following motivations:

- Theft of financial data or personal information that they can sell
- Encryption of data and then demand a ransom for the decryption keys
- Recruitment of systems into their botnets.

Malware writers usually work alone or in small groups. Their malware targets Windows systems but more recently cross-platform malware has appeared. Malware writers favour a scattergun approach trying to target and spread to as many systems as possible using whatever vulnerability they understand. Malware writers often revise their software so that new variants of their malware use different vulnerabilities and try to subvert antivirus programs.

Script Kiddies

Script kiddies have the most basic of technical skills. They download hacking tools developed by more skilled hackers and malware writers using attacks they don't fully understand. Although they are the least skilled, they are the most prevalent. If you attach a system to the Internet and monitor for attacks, you will see it comes under attack daily, and these attacks are easily recognised by most intrusion detection systems. I have separated them from hackers because of their differing skill levels and the fact that script kiddie attacks occur more often.

Script kiddies are usually motivated by the following:

- Boredom: they have nothing to do so are mischievous.

- Showing off: they and their friends have poor IT skills and want to show off to one another.

Script kiddies scan the Internet for vulnerable systems using their automated tools. Their technical skill is often very limited and this can be even more of a concern as they do not understand what they are doing, leading to them damaging systems accidentally. Script kiddies favour the more current and fashionable tools.

Journalists

Often, journalists aren't considered a threat to an IT system and in the traditional sense they aren't. What I mean by this is that usually a journalist won't attack the system online. What they do though is physically compromise the system. Journalists usually have very limited technical skills unless they enlist the help of someone else. A physical compromise is favoured as they can gather evidence to support their aims.

These aims are usually one of the following:

- Public interest
- Big-selling story
- To build their reputation.

Journalists do have some exemptions under the Data Protection Act but they must still comply with the computer misuse act; this is another reason for favouring physical compromise rather than a cyber attack. Journalists often use undercover techniques, for example posing as a cleaner or some other staff member to gain physical access. This threat poses a very interesting vector and may motivate some organisations to carry out background checks on all staff they employ.

Criminals

Criminals should not be confused with hackers or malware writers. Although all these threats commit crimes, criminals' motivations and techniques are different. A criminal is often trying to subvert the process or service that the IT system itself supplies, for example buying something using someone else's payment details. This is a different threat to consider because we need to look at not only how the technology we build can be compromised but also what we build.

A criminal's motivation is the most basic:

- Financial gain
- Support for other crimes.

The scariest thing about criminals is that although their motivation is the most basic, it is also the strongest. The financial motivation coupled with the lack of morals makes this a very daunting threat and often criminals will not rule out any attack vector if the rewards are great enough. This means that they may not only attack the system online but also favour a physical compromise of the system.

Physical Intruder

The best way to think about a physical intruder is to think about a typical burglar: someone who has broken in with the intention of theft of the physical assets rather than the information itself. IT equipment is often very valuable and easily sells on sites such as eBay. Fortunately server and rack equipment is large and not easy to steal, so this may lead to the physical intruder stealing things such as copper cabling that can be sold for profit. A physical intrusion may occur even if there is nothing of value at the location; some intruders may do so on the off chance of finding something of value.

Physical intruders are motivated by the following:

- Financial gain
- Potential financial gain.

Physical intruders usually are not motivated by the value of the data but more the value of the physical systems. This can lead to the risk of the compromise being miscalculated as people tend to only consider the value of the information they are protecting and not the physical infrastructure.

Researchers

Researchers is a strange one that most people often do not consider. A researcher becomes more of a problem as the profile of your organisation rises. Take Facebook as an example: its website comes under daily scrutiny from those trying to find security vulnerabilities, and their motivation can vary greatly. Some do so to receive payment for a bug bounty, and some do it to produce a paper or other research that they want to present. Whatever their motivation these researchers are often the best equipped to target your system. This is because they have a great technical knowledge and have selected your system for a reason, usually because they believe they will be successful.

Researches are typically motivated by the following:

- Fame: publishing their findings and receiving credit

- Money: payment either from a bug bounty or the sale of their findings, perhaps to a journalist
- Pure research: for a dissertation or other research.

A researcher usually only goes as far as to find the vulnerabilities within your system; they won't actually exploit them. A researcher typically wants to stay on the right side of the law so will be keen not to break any. The researcher may even inform you of their findings before publication, so it is important that you take the time to respond and act on their findings before publication. A lot of the impact on the organisation can be mitigated if the researcher asserts that their finds have since been fixed.

Hacktivists

Hacktivists have become more and more prevalent over the last few years with groups such as Lulzsec and Anonymous now an active threat. These groups comprise people who have hacking skills but are motivated by some moral goal. They typically target government organisations or organisations with ties to government. They may, depending on your business, target yourself; for example, Greenpeace has been accused of hacking oil companies.

Hacktivists have the following motivations:

- Public awareness of their cause
- An effective means of protesting their views.

The technical skills of hacktivists are limited and they focus on disruption rather than breaking into a system and stealing data. Denial-of-service (DoS) attacks are their preferred method of disruption. DOS attacks overload the target with too much data so that the system is so preoccupied with the data being fired at it that it doesn't have the capacity to service legitimate users. Such attacks can be more of an annoyance unless you are relying on your website for your core business. The motivations of hacktivists can change overnight, so it is important to be aware of any changes in society that may motivate them to target your organisation.

Disgruntled Employees

Often our own employees are overlooked as a threat. It's a cliché to say that our staff are our strongest and weakest control with regard to security. In this case it is a double loss, as not only are they a weakness but they are also possibly an active threat to the system. Disgruntled employees typically pose two threats: deliberately compromising our system, or because of their lack of engagement they are more prone to errors. Reasons why a member of staff could become disgruntled range from a disagreement over pay to being overworked. It is important that an organisation is aware of morale levels within the workforce and steps are taken to improve it where needed.

Disgruntled employees typically have the following motivations:

- Revenge
- Lack of interest/pride in their work.

Disgruntled employees will aim to damage the organisation's reputation rather than compromise a system for financial reasons. This can be done through an information leak or affecting the availability of a system.

CHAPTER 5: QUICK AND DIRTY RISK ASSESSMENT

Chapter Overview

There are many risk assessment processes, but many are long and overly complicated. More and more organisations are moving to a more agile working environment, developing systems iteratively, changing functionality to meet the users' requirements. This sort of working can make it very difficult to follow a complex risk management process. Traditionally these processes have been written favouring a waterfall development methodology.

In the modern digital age organisations need to be flexible to take advantage of opportunities as they present themselves. Depending on the organisation's culture and risk appetite the decision on whether to proceed with a new service may depend on the outcome of a risk assessment. Following a traditional method may be too slow, meaning the organisation either misses the opportunity or proceeds without any knowledge of the risks.

Giving a small amount of risk advice rapidly is more enabling to the business than a lot of risk advice slowly. This is the reason why I have included this chapter, as it includes a lightweight, easily understandable risk process that can be applied quickly.

Objectives

In this chapter you will learn the following:

- How to identify risks
- How to categorise and prioritise risks.

Identifying Risks

Identifying risks can often be very difficult, as people's minds move to the more traditional technical exploits and vulnerabilities. In the real world you have to think beyond the technology; there is the insider threat or even the process itself could be exploited. When identifying risks I use four categories: Internal, External, Process and Technical. These can be described as the following:

Internal: risks that are posed internally. This can be either from other internal systems or staff members. Examples of internal risks could be user error while administering the system, or if our system is reliant upon another system that is due to undergo maintenance. The defining factor of an internal risk is that its occurrence is within our control.

External: risks that are posed externally. This can include external systems that we are reliant upon or staff employed by service providers that we rely upon. Also included are acts of god or terrorism. Examples could be our internet service provider accidentally cuts us off or our data centre could be flooded.

Process: risks related to the process and operation of the system itself. This can include risks around the functionality provided by the system itself. Examples include weak passwords that can be guessed or the ability to fraudulently carry out a transaction.

Technology: risks that relate to the technology employed. These risks relate directly to the technology stack itself and how it is configured. Examples include the lack of a firewall on a network, missing antivirus or a weak cipher.

When identifying risks you should first document the system fully (*Chapter 7*), then work through each point of that system asking if there could be risks around Internal, External, Process or Technology factors. When deciding if there is a potential risk you should also refer to your threat sources and identify which of those would look to exploit that risk. This will help you identify which risks are most likely to happen because more threats exist in that area. More importantly it gives your risks context when discussing them with technical and management teams; you will be able to say who would exploit that risk. Risks that people can relate to in the real world are easier to communicate and will be taken more seriously.

Defining the Risk Level

Once our risks are identified we need some way of prioritising them. It is extremely unlikely that we will have an unlimited amount of money or time to fix all the risks found. In fact, if you are working on a highly sensitive project that does afford the time and resources to build a secure system then you should follow this process up with a more formal risk assessment.

There are two key parts to prioritising a risk: likelihood and severity. Likelihood is a measure of the chances of a risk occurring and how often it may happen. Severity deals with how severe the consequences would be if the attack were successful. By scoring the likelihood of a risk happening and its severity if successful we can rank the risk as low, medium or high. This is a very crude method of risk categorisation but it is rapid, and we are trying to be agile.

Severity

The severity has five ratings:

1. Extremely low
2. Low
3. Medium
4. High
5. Extremely high.

The next section describes these ratings, and includes example risks that could fall into each of these categories. Also, depending on your organisation you may want to realign the costs so that they better fit the size of the organisation.

Extremely Low: the impact of the breach is small as only informational data was stolen or corrupted. The remediation cost was small and mainly cost staff time to investigate.

Such attacks include:

- Port scan
- Identify active IPs and protocols.

Low: the impact of the breach is still small as only a small amount of non-sensitive data was stolen or corrupted. The remediation cost is still small and mainly only staff time was lost investigating the breach.

Such attacks include:

- Interception of non-sensitive data, for example a BBC news page
- Minor denial-of-service attack (noticed by network team but not users).

Medium: the attack was successful in stealing or compromising valuable data, although not sensitive. The system needs investment to conduct a full investigation and possibly new controls implemented, costing thousands of pounds.

Such attacks include:

- Theft of password hashes
- Theft of account names
- Denial-of-service noticed by users.

High: the system has been severely breached with large amounts of data stolen, including sensitive. The reputation of the organisation has been damaged and remediation work will cost millions of pounds.

Such attacks include:

- Theft of passwords
- User accounts compromised (although not root)
- Denial-of-service so that the service is unavailable.

Extremely high: the system has been completely compromised, and the service is no longer available or has had to be shut down. The reputation of the organisation is in tatters and work to remediate the breach will cost tens of millions of pounds.

Such attacks include:

- Root access achieved
- Breach of data protection laws.

Likelihood

Likelihood is applied in much the same way – how often would a threat source look to attack our system using the methods defined in one of our risks? The following list describes the frequency of attack:

- Less than once a year
- At least once a year
- At least once every six months
- At least once a month
- At least once a week.

Risk Table

	Minor Disruption to A	Minor Disruption to IC	Disruption to CIA	Loss of personal data	Complete system loss
Less than once a year	Very Low	Very Low	Low	Medium Low	Medium
At least once a year	Very Low	Low	Medium Low	Medium	Medium High
At least once every six months	Low	Medium Low	Medium	Medium High	High
At least once a month	Medium Low	Medium	Medium High	High	Critical
At least once a week	Medium	Medium High	High	Critical	Critical

Realigning the Risk Level

You may be wondering at this point about the data that is to be hosted on the system and the impact if it is breached. It seems common sense that more sensitive data would have a higher risk category and non-sensitive data would have a lower risk category. However, unless you wish to compare risks from two separate systems then the realignment exercise is pointless as all risks would increase or decrease by the same amount. Instead, when discussing the risks I recommend setting the context of the risk be defining how critical the asset is. This can then drive the discussion on what risks we will fix, so, for high-risk systems we may want to fix all risks from low and above, and for low-risk systems we may only want to fix high risks and above.

CHAPTER 6: GETTING BUY-IN FROM YOUR PEERS

Rationale: Lots of books discuss how to get management buy-in. In the context of this book you already have management buy-in because they're either reading this book or you've been employed by management and they're paying your wages. Often it is other IT professionals who need to be won over. They often see security as a barrier and look to go around that barrier rather than engage properly with security. Any good security professional must have buy-in from their peers, as without it you cannot implement effective security controls.

Content: This chapter discusses how to get buy-in from your peers so they understand the security risks to their system and how you can help them. This can be done by showing and demonstrating to them penetration test results; these people are technically minded so reproducing the risk in practice really helps. Secondly, these teams have sat through many (probably annually) boring and generic security awareness presentations. Instead, tailor these presentations to them, as this shows you understand their area and, their risks and problems. This approach will increase engagement during the presentation and outside during day to day work. I also discuss some of the most common IT teams you will find in a business and advise on how to better engage with them and the value you can offer.

Chapter Overview

Having buy-in from your peers benefits everyone. There's nothing worse than a project being considerably delayed or even cancelled because of an early decision that later turned out to be a bad one. The earlier in the project everyone gets together and considers the security implications, the better. Gaining this inclusion can only be done through buy-in from your peers. Achieve this and you will be included earlier in projects.

Gaining this buy-in is not a quick or easy process. Often security is seen as a blocker or a necessary evil at the end (some organisations are better than others). The best way to build relationships and get buy-in is to include people in security decisions. When people know that their input is valued and that they can help steer the security of the project they are more likely to buy in.

This chapter discusses techniques I have used to get buy-in from my peers. It explains the usefulness of each technique and how it can be implemented. As with security controls I recommend using more than one technique as success is more likely. It also means you engage with technical and non-technical staff members. Also included are some of the key teams needed to deliver and manage a secure project.

Objectives

In this chapter you will learn the following:

- How to get technical teams to attack and understand the system
- How to raise security awareness
- How to engage with specific peer groups.

Points of Contact with your Peers

Scoping penetration tests

The penetration test is often one of the most interesting parts of the security assurance process for technical team members. This is due to two key aspects: the competition of whether someone else can break the system we have built, and the certain attraction of 'hacking' and breaking into systems.

The first step when scoping a penetration test should be asking the technical team how they would attack the system. No one is going to know the system better than the people who built it, so by documenting how they believe it can be attacked we can ensure not only that the test is more thorough but also take the first step of engagement. I recommend holding a workshop, put the high-level designs on the wall, and work through each component, discuss its weaknesses and document them. These attacks can then be included in the full penetration test (*Chapter 9*).

Penetration test results

Penetration test results are great for not only engaging with your peers but also learning. Penetration tests are technical processes; even when they document a security hole that they have found, only the technical team will truly understand what is happening in the underlying system. The technical team is usually responsible for fixing the security holes, so we need to ensure they fully understand the attacks. I recommend holding a meeting with the team to discuss the report. The technical team will understand the system they have built but it is unlikely that they will understand all the attacks detailed in the document. Even better, if your budget allows, arrange for the penetration test team to hold a workshop with the technical team. Have them demonstrate each attack showing the code and scripts they used, allowing the technical team to see the attacks and work with the penetration test team to analyse each finding, this will further the team's understanding of the security controls in the system and of security in general. Also, this kind of workshop can be fun, as people enjoy the technical challenge.

Security awareness

Security awareness is typically the most common way of interacting with staff but often these annual awareness sessions are death by PowerPoint and really of little use. When I run an awareness session I look back at the previous 12 months and look at security incidents that have affected the organisation and the stories that have been big in the media. The most important part of awareness is making the information useful to staff, something they can apply in their day to day roles. Sometimes when working I'll be stopped in the corridor by a peer who mentions a recent security breach in the news; they want to know more and if we are protected. Another useful inclusion is to discuss the threat landscape and the current threats to the organisation. Get peers involved, show them the real risks to the organisation and show them what is currently worrying you as a security professional.

Security awareness doesn't have to be an annual event where you save a year's worth of learning for one presentation. Smaller weekly or monthly newsletters can be very effective in keeping staff up to date, especially on current news stories or even recent security incidents that have occurred in the organisation. These events remind people of their responsibilities. For example, in my organisation when we see an upturn in the amount of phishing email being received by staff we issue a newsletter to all staff explaining what's going on. We direct them to the policy and processes to manage phishing emails and try to safely include examples of the actual emails being received by the organisation.

Another great way to raise awareness is with project awareness sessions. At the start of a project make sure everyone has the same amount of baseline information. If you can conduct a quick and dirty risk assessment (*Chapter 5*) early on in the project then you can use that as the basis for an awareness session. Conducting these sessions is also a great way to introduce yourself to the project team and show them that you are adopting a proactive approach to security. Attendees can raise their concerns so that you may consider them early.

System operating procedure creation

System operating procedure (SyOps) documents are a great place to put in writing how staff will properly and securely operate a system. If you create SyOps without consulting those who it will apply to then you're likely to upset a lot of people and achieve the opposite to engagement. However, if you can bring the knowledge of those who it will apply to on board then not only will you create better, more secure SyOps but also people will be more inclined to actually follow them. In the creation of a new SyOp first conduct a risk assessment in partnership with the people who it will apply to. Take the time to understand how they work and show them the risks (if any) posed by their current working practices. These risks can then drive discussion about how things can be done better. Allow those who the procedure applies to to develop the procedure by letting them make the decisions on how they want to work. If the group doesn't agree or understand the controls then they are unlikely to follow them.

How to Engage with your Peers

Software development

The software development team are likely the most technical team, and used to creating innovative solutions to problems. They typically enjoy the challenge of learning new technology. However, often they dislike having to follow formal and administrative processes.

The best way to engage with software developers is to work with them on the more technical aspects of security. Including them in the penetration testing process is a great way of harnessing their creativity and technical understanding while ensuring the effectiveness of the penetration testing process.

I have taken this a step further and worked with software developers to help them create their own security testing scripts to penetration test their own code. If you do go down this route then I still recommend procuring a third-party penetration tester service to verify the results.

Help Desk

The help desk is responsible for handing day to day user

support, and beyond technology they are often the first team to notice if a system is under attack. This is because often the users of a system will notice if something is wrong, for example slow loading, account changes or even missing data; the user will then contact a help desk for support. The help desk has an overall view of a system's performance and its current state, which means if a high number of users report a slow system then there is probably something wrong and it needs to be investigated. The key question for the help desk is whether the current issues are part of a much larger security problem or whether users just do not understand the system.

Help desk staff are usually not the most technical of people. Their skills are in communication and remaining calm even when confronted by the angriest of customers. Because of this I recommend going through security awareness processes with them. By ensuring they understand the threat landscape to the organisation and current security trends they are more likely to spot a security breach and escalate than simply put it down to user error. A good strategy is to pass them small amounts of security awareness information on a regular basis. This ensures security is always at the forefront of their work and also that they can better serve customers.

Business Analysts

Business analysts are often the least technical members of the team but typically understand the most about the business, and possibly the users depending on their roles. Business analysts help us understand our users, so it's important they are engaged with security to build that relationship. Another key area of engagement is that they can help manage user expectations. For example, often customers like links to be sent in emails, but we all know that scammers use emails with links to infect users or even direct them to a spoof web page to steal their credentials. If we ensure business analysts understand some of these common attacks, we can better work with the users to strike a balance of security and usability.

For business analysts I recommend not only general annual security awareness sessions but also specific awareness sessions for the project they are about to undertake. Any sort of awareness needs to focus on the process side of security. I once delivered a session to business analysts on the sensitivity of different data and how the aggregation of lots of small data leaks can result in a large data breach. The aim of the analyst shouldn't be to solve security problems, just ensure the topic is discussed and considered through the analysis process.

Management

If you find yourself in an organisation that does not have a high regard for security then you're never going to change that without buy-in from the top. Unfortunately, if the organisation's culture isn't security conscious then it is probably management that have fostered this negative culture. Opening their eyes to the risks that they face will not be easy, but a good start would be to use some fear, uncertainty and doubt (FUD). These are scare stories, often used effectively by sales people to sell a new secure IT product. Choose stories that have recently been in the media, stories about security breaches and other similar events. Break down these stories into plain and simple English, explain how they impacted the business and the cost and reputational damage that they caused. If you have recently undergone a penetration test and have similar examples that exist in your own systems, even better. Showing them that your own organisation is equally as vulnerable should force them to take security more seriously.

CHAPTER 7: DOCUMENTING THE SYSTEM FOR EVERYONE

Rationale: Systems have many technical designs that IT teams use to develop and maintain the system. However, these systems are very hard to understand for members of staff who are not technical, typically management. This can be a real barrier for management, especially when they need to make a key decision based on risk.

Content: To help management understand the system you can re-document the system into a kind of entity relationship diagram. This diagram will be a high-level view of staff, networks, systems and so on, and each entity will be connected with an arrow showing the flow of information and control points in the system. This diagram is even more useful when some entities are outside of the business' control, for example customers or Cloud suppliers. Additionally this diagram can show where risks exist, to help decide where the most security controls are needed. The diagrams also help scope better penetration tests of the system, making sure our tests mimic the risks and cover all aspects of the system. This chapter features my own example of an e-commerce system fully designed using this method; the design includes all parts of the system, including developers, users, the network and so on.

Chapter Overview

One of the biggest obstacles is helping the business understand what the system looks like. Often their understanding is limited to the database, network and perhaps the web pages that provide the system interface. The truth is systems are far more complicated when we consider them from a risk point of view. I have often found a gulf between the technical diagrams provided by a system designer or architect and the technical understanding of the business. I have seen this gulf cause many problems in meetings where a lack of common understanding has meant subjects had to be revisited or people didn't correctly understand the risk to the system, sometimes feeding their paranoia or giving a false sense of security. In this chapter I show how a system can be documented in a common, simple way. This technique not only allows the business to understand the system but also gives them the ability to collaborate with technical staff.

Objectives

In this chapter you will learn the following:

- How to document a high-level view of an entire system
- How to show control boundaries
- Showing the risks and where they exist in the system.

Setting the Scene

Before showing a diagram I need to set the scene for the system we are going to document. I have imagined the following scenario: I am working for an e-commerce start-up, which is looking to create its first online store that will allow them to sell their wares but also allow third-party sellers to also sell using their platform. The following basic requirements have been put together:

1. Customers must be able to purchase various items using card payments.

2. The website must be Cloud based so that it can scale quickly.
3. The database for the system must remain in house so that our team can administer it.
4. Third parties must be able to also add items to the database to sell.

Entities

Before we document the system we need to think about the things or entities that are involved (please don't call this an entity relationship diagram, your database colleagues will hate you) in the system. This should include everything: systems, hardware, software, people, locations and sometimes processes. Add anything you think is key to showing on your system for an interaction. For our example let's think about some of the entities:

1. Amazon web services (AWS) based within the EU.

   AWS meets our Cloud requirement to allow us to scale quickly. They also have data centres within the EU, which is important as this means the Data Protection Act must be followed. I consider this a key point for two reasons: it gives some assurance as to how our data in their possession will be treated, and it is a regulatory rule that we must abide by as our service will be hosted within the EU.

2. Website, hosted on AWS with an API into our network to query the internal database.

   This item is key as our e-commerce site will effectively be split in two, with the web pages themselves sitting on AWS so that they can scale up if our service proves popular. Our database that will contain all the items for sale will remain on our network so it's within our control. This type of design pattern is a great example of something that can confuse and worry a business person. Often they will be worried that the system is in the possession of a third party and will question whether that third party has the same levels of security. Remember this point as it will translate well in the diagram we draw later.

3. Customers, who could be anywhere in the world connecting to our website via the Internet.

   This is very obvious for anyone who understands the web, but it's a key point to display for anyone who doesn't understand the web. The Internet is involved and we need to understand what is connected to it and what is under our control.

4. Card payments carried out by third-party SagePay via the web.

   Our company is a start-up that needs to process card payments. If we wanted to do this ourselves then we would have to comply with the Payment Card Industry Data Security Standard (the PCI DSS). At this stage this would be a heavy and resource-taxing effort, so outsourcing this requirement to a third party is an ideal choice. This is a key point we want to show in our diagram so that people understand where the customers will pay and where card transactions will actually take place.

5. Third-party sellers who can connect to a private web portal hosted internally by us.

   This is an important process not only from a business point of view but also a security one. Any time data can be accessed or changed, risk is introduced to our system. For this requirement there is no need for the service to be Cloud hosted, and there are a few reasons for this. From a business point of view our third-party suppliers are not likely to increase as quickly as our customers, therefore we don't need to scale quickly. From a security point of view this is a sensitive service, as changes will be made to our products' database. If this service was provided on our AWS instance, then if AWS is compromised the entire system is lost as the attacker would be able to change the database and control what our customers see. Because of this risk the common sense approach is to split and host this service separately. If we host this service internally we cannot only control the service but also the connection to it, offering us a higher degree of assurance. Again, this is another key function that we need to display. If customers and third parties are both accessing a web page of some sort then people may assume they are accessing the same service. By documenting this in our diagram we can show a clear separation and explain the risk we are mitigating.

6. Our network that is provided by us and has an Internet connection.

   We need to show what is connected to our network and how many systems it is connected to. This is important from a security point of view as we need to understand where sensitive systems are connected and where our boundaries are. If in our example we had one flat network that allowed customers to connect into, potentially we are exposing ourselves to the entire Internet for attack.

7. Our own web developers and database administrators as well as our own network administrators.

   Most diagrams include customers or users but not the people involved in running and creating the system. That's just insane, since in terms of fully understanding the system you are building you need to include your own people. Of course some common sense needs to be applied, and I wouldn't expect to see literally every person, but for this example the web developers, the database administrators and our network administrators should be shown. Web developers are interesting for this example as they interact with the database API and the web pages on the AWS instance. That is because they code and deploy both. If we worked in a larger company then we may have separate teams (from a security perspective this would be better as a segregation of duty) for the web pages and the database API; our diagram would change to reflect that.

Service Overview

Based on the preceding requirements I have put together a service overview diagram. I call it a service overview because the diagram shows much more than just systems and people. Also, you can create one of these diagrams for your wider systems to show connections, but they work best when only showing a single service or subset of systems.

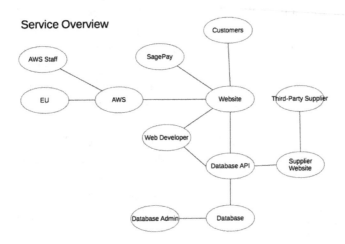

The preceding diagram is a first draft of all the entities and their interactions. It should give a good idea of who and what interacts with who and what. One of the first things you'll notice is that I haven't included the Internet or our network. Both of these things by their nature connect things, so if I include them then a number of the entities will be connected and it gets messy. The other problem is that strictly speaking, our customers connect to the Internet and then our website, and our website connects to our database API also via the Internet. If I drew the diagram to show this then it would cause confusion and some people may think the customer is actually connecting to our database API over the web; this is simply not the case. This blurry line is also repeated in a similar way for our third-party suppliers as they would connect to the web and then to our network via the Internet, causing another mess in our diagram. For the moment, put aside the fact that the Internet and our network are missing; I show you how to add those to the diagram in a moment. For now I will explain the connections and why they are connected in the diagram in the way that they are.

From top left, AWS is connected to AWS staff and EU. Amazon is a US company, so a business person's first thought could be that the firm's data will reside in the US; including EU clarifies things. It also clarifies which legal jurisdiction the data resides under. A question you may now have is where are our systems and network and shouldn't we specify where they will be located? Typically they will be with the business, so if you're UK based then they will probably be UK hosted; a business person will probably also make this assumption. Only include locations where they vary to that of the core business, but whether you take this down to city level rather than national level is up to you. AWS also has a connection to its staff. It is important to include this so we can see what other people will have access to on the cloud systems hosting our data and possibly even our information itself. This is even more key if those staff reside in a separate place to the system they are supporting. The next key entity is our website, which is connected to AWS because this is where it is hosted. It is also connected to SagePay, Customers, Web Developers and our Database API. The connection to SagePay is an important one as they are the ones who will carry out card payments on our behalf. A card payment process could have been added in between SagePay and our Website to clarify this, but seek feedback or assess how people interpret the diagram before adding this. If I were to add it then Card Payment would sit between SagePay and the Website entities. The next key part is the connection to our customers, as this clearly shows the part of the service they will connect to and clarifies that they will not connect to any of our internally hosted systems. The Database API is next on the list and this separation shows how the website will connect to our internal services as well as the split in the user interface and the business logic. I mentioned earlier that these two systems are split, one being on AWS and the other being internally hosted on our network. The diagram doesn't yet show this division, but I will show you that soon. We now have our Web Developers, who are added to show that they are the ones building and deploying the Website and the Database API. You may want to divide this duty so that vulnerabilities aren't introduced into both systems; however, for us it's the same team and the diagram accurately reflects the reliance on this team. The next part is the Supplier Website and Third-party Suppliers, which has two key parts: the separation from the customer website and AWS, and the connection to the Database API. Again, the diagram doesn't accurately show that the system resides on our own internal network, and this is covered later. The final part of the diagram is the Database and the Database Administrators. The database is our most valuable asset as this is where all the stock is logged and where the third-party sellers will add their own stock. The connection to the Database API is a key one as this shows that there isn't a direct link to our database; an assumption can be made that the API is used to control access and therefore is a control to protect the database itself. The final key link is to the database administrators. This team are trusted to protect our key asset and are possibly the most important group from the point of view of supporting the service.

Adding Boundaries

It was obvious from the last section that this diagram needed to show Internet-connected services and our own internal network ones. So let's add them.

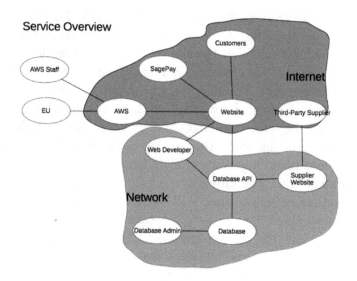

So from top left let's work through our diagram again and understand why what entity sits where and why.

AWS Cloud, like most cloud services is internet connected and this is often the only way to connect to these types of services. Their staff sit outside of this location because for my example Amazon's staff administer the machines directly not over the Internet, hence the direct link. The key part of the diagram is that our website itself is within the Internet zone because it is hosted and accessed from the Internet. Customers can access the website via the Internet and at no point is one of our internal systems directly used by the customer. SagePay is also accessed over the Internet. The payment service sits on the web and connects directly with our website, meaning that at no point do we handle payment details. Next is our third-party supplier, which also connects over the Internet but the difference is that they access a supplier website that is hosted on our own internal network. The next interesting point (or maybe concern) is that our web developers are building systems in both the Internet and the more trusted network zone. I say concern because they potentially provide a bridge between the two zones now because they work with systems on both sides.

Showing Information Flow

At this stage we understand the key entities in our system and where these entities reside. We have a good understanding of what entity interacts with what so we understand the system from a high-level point of view. The next stage is to add information flow. Not all flows of information are two-way, for example the web developer's information flow with the website is one way. They create the website and then deploy it, which is a single-direction flow. It is important to understand the direction of the flows so that we know where information resides and can understand the risks. For example, where information flows out of a system we need to know where it's going. The same as when information flows into a system, we need to ensure that access is allowed; an untrusted system should not be connecting to a trusted system and taking information out. Instead we have a trusted system push information out to an untrusted system, assuming we want the information to go that way.

I have amended the following diagram to show those information flows:

Service Overview

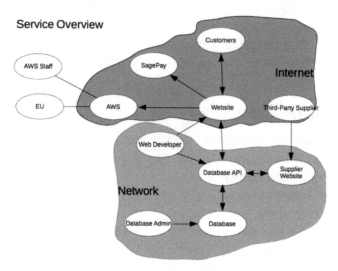

This time I will start from the customer and work my way down. The customer typically provides us registration and search information, and the system responds by displaying products it has retrieved from the Database API. The next flow is the flow to SagePay, which is a single-directional flow; via our own website the customer provides payment details. It is important that this flow is single directional so that data cannot be taken from the SagePay system via the website. Then we come to the web developer: their two single-flow interactions are developing and then deploying the website and database API. This is single flow because they don't retrieve any information from the systems once created and deployed. Our third-party suppliers provide information only in the form of items for sale but they don't actually receive any information back. They receive their output from the finance department in the form of invoices and payments so for the scope of our IT system they don't actually receive any input. From a security point of view this is good because they are connecting into our network, and would be in a good position to exfiltrate data. The

Database API is kind of working as a router, as it has data flowing into it and it is retrieving and sending that data back. From a security point of view it is one of the most sensitive services because of this function. If the Database API is compromised then the attacker can change or steal data from the database. I recommend splitting the database API into a customer and supplier API so that the systems have more granular specific functions. For example, the supplier API needs the ability to update the database but the user one doesn't. The final set of flows are around the database, the database admins and the two-way flow of data between the Database API and the database. We know data flows to and from the database as it allows itself to be updated and serves information out for the customer. The database admin themselves only add information to the database as they support and configure it.

Adding the Threats

The final step is to add the threats to the system. In *Chapter 4* we identified the threats and looked at how they could attack the system. Now we will map those threats onto the system so that we can better understand where and how they can attack the system. Adding all the threats to the diagram means we can see what parts of the system are most likely to be attacked and therefore ensure we spend more time and effort securing those parts of the system. For the next example I have picked four threats and mapped them to the diagram hackers, fraudsters, rivals and insiders.

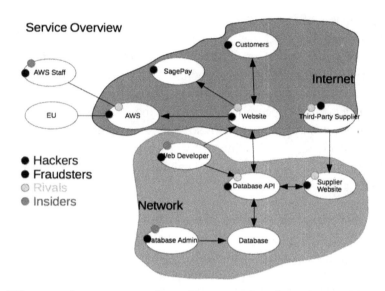

We now have a complete diagram showing the entities, how they link together and the direction of those interfaces. We have finally added the threats so at this stage we have a very good view of the risks posed to the system. Rather than working through the diagram I will explain this diagram from the threats' point of view and suggest mitigations. I have added threats to each entity from the point of view of what they would be able to attack rather than what they would like to attack. So, for example, a hacker can't just attack the database; they need to compromise the Database API first and then attack the database. When securing the system, time would be taken to secure the database so that a compromise to an edge service wouldn't mean compromise to a deeper service.

I have added hackers to all systems that have an Internet connection, therefore allowing them to attack via the web. SagePay would be their primary target as this service takes card payments and would provide data of the most value to them in the form of card details and personal information. By having SagePay process the payments we have transferred this risk to them. Next on the list is AWS. Hackers will look to target this service regardless of whether we used it or not. Compromising this platform would allow them to further compromise other services that were deployed upon it. As with SagePay we have transferred this risk to Amazon. Our website will be targeted by hackers, first and foremost so that they can steal the personal information provided through registration and secondly so that they can use it as a platform to attack deeper services. In terms of sensitivity the Database API is the most sensitive service that we expose to the Internet, as it controls data in and out, and control of this service would almost certainly mean complete compromise. I would split this service so that a customer read-only version was exposed to the Internet. A separate update service for the supplier website would also be created, and this would not have a connection to the Internet, therefore mitigating the hacker threat. The supplier website is the least likely to be attacked by a hacker because it represents the least value to them in terms of what they can steal. This service is kept on our internal network because of the large impact its compromise would have.

I have marked fraudsters against those entities that represent people. I have not marked them against technical systems as if they attacked those I would consider them hackers. It's important for your system to be clear about what each threat can do and how they could attack the system. My fraudster wants to compromise the system but by using social engineering attempts, for example getting staff to share login details or pretending to be a legitimate customer in order to gain access. The fraudsters may even consider threats of bribes to achieve their goals. I have included fraudsters to show that it's not just the technical aspects of the system that could be compromised.

If you are selling an online commerce service, what better way to get new customers than to take down your rivals? Your rival's site goes down and so their customers come to you; the law of averages says that if you provide a good service then you will retain some of those customers. Our suppliers also have rivals who wish to compromise their service, therefore I have added this threat not only to our website but also to AWS. I haven't added rivals to SagePay because I would hope that financial institutions don't make a habit of attacking one another. In terms of protecting against this threat I suggest using anti-DDOS technology or perhaps even Cloud hosting services. As for your suppliers who are targeted, either ensure they have a high service level with penalties or make sure you can move suppliers quickly.

The final threat are insiders, perhaps the scariest threat given the havoc they could cause. I previously mentioned segregation of duties for web developers as they create the website and the Database API and this threat is exactly why you would want that divide. They could compromise the entire system, or they could only compromise part of it; we would hope that the second team would spot the compromise to the other part of the system. Insider threats will always exist as long as your staff can be bribed or threatened, or even if they are not totally happy in their jobs. Background checks and thorough auditing can help mitigate this threat by ensuring people are trustworthy and they know their attack will be detected.

CHAPTER 8: MAPPING DATA IN THE SYSTEM

Chapter Overview

Ask why a system needs to be secure and the answer will almost always be the data that resides on that system. Add in the fact that most services consist of more than one system and we can assume that our data could reside in multiple places and we may have more than one dataset with a different level of value. So if it's the data we are trying to protect and it may be in more than one place then it makes sense that we need to map where it is. This chapter uses a similar technique to the previous chapter so I recommend reading that first.

Understanding the location of data is important when considering where the threats are. If multiple threats could attack a service with data that is sensitive then that service needs to be further secured. If a service contains level-sensitive data then we may choose to live with the risks, but unless we know the value of the information and where it is we won't know which parts of the system to secure.

This chapter shows you a simple technique to document where the data is and understand where more than one dataset may reside together.

Objectives

In this chapter you will learn the following:

- How to map data in your system.

Mapping Data

You can map data by following a similar technique to modelling our threats. To keep the diagram concise you will need a separate diagram. As such I have removed the threat actors from the previous diagram in *Chapter 7* and added the data locations:

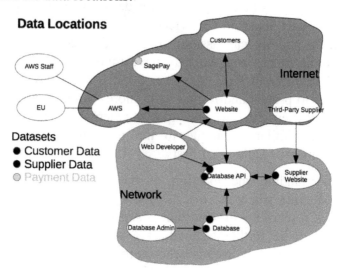

As with the threats diagram I have added markers to show where data not only resides but also passes through. Remember that data in transit is just as much at risk as data at rest. Why hack the database when you can tap the website and intercept the data before it is sent to the database? For this example I identified three key datasets: Customer data, Supplier data and Payment data.

Customer data is all data relating to the customer, such as identity information and order details (excluding card details) including things like wish lists and viewed data. This data is first entered into the website, which is then sent to the Database API where it is sent to be stored in the database. In terms of logic I would expect some basic validation to be done on the website so details are complete and the right length and so on. The real validation comes from the Database API where checks ensure no duplication and that details are valid, for example address details actually exist. Customer data is sensitive in that it identifies a citizen and is considered personal data, which means it is protected by the Data Protection Act.

Supplier data is all data relating to the supplier, so details about the specific supplier but also information about the items they want to sell. These details much like customer data undergo simple website validation before being passed to the Database API for more intensive processing and validation before being stored in the database. This data is less sensitive because item details are public information anyway as they are publicly accessible. Supplier details are also less sensitive as these details are often in the public domain since the company will want to raise its public profile.

Payment data is data relating to the card payments for website transactions. This data only resides with SagePay; customers enter the data directly into SagePay and do not enter payment data into our website before we send it off for processing. This data model makes this very clear and ensures the PCI DSS regulations do not apply to us.

The payment details are the least of my concern because they are separate and never come into our possession. The other two datasets do concern me, however, especially where they reside on the same system in the Database API and Database. The aggregation of these datasets makes these two systems tempting targets and means they need further protection. Moreover, as I suggested in *Chapter 7* we may want a separate Customer and Supplier database API system. Had we not completed this exercise we would not have realised that.

CHAPTER 9: PENETRATION TESTING

Chapter Overview

Poor penetration testing frustrates me, and I have come across a few organisations that fail to get the basics right. Good penetration testing offers a high degree of assurance that the systems you have implemented have been done so securely, but you only get this assurance if your testing is thorough. This chapter starts with explaining the difference between white box and black box. Both tests have their pros and cons, so it's important to know what these are so that you can select the right sort of testing. I also explain the sorts of tests you can do, which range from traditional penetration testing to build reviews and vulnerability assessments. Penetration testing doesn't just have to include the usual attempted attack (hack) that we are accustomed to; we can tailor our testing to suit our needs and budget. Finally I discuss what to do after the test results are received. The most important thing when looking at the penetration test report is to add your own system knowledge to the reports, as the Critical to Low risk label findings usually given will not be effective in managing the fixes.

Objectives

In this chapter you will learn the following:

- The different types of test
- Different ways to test security
- How to scope a penetration test
- What to do with the results.

Types of Penetration Test

There are many types of penetration test, each with a varying degree of complexity, expense and time requirements. They include the following:

- White box testing
- Black box testing
- Vulnerability test
- Build review
- Code review
- Physical assessment.

White box testing

White box testing is arguably the most efficient and effective form of testing. It involves providing the tester with design and process documents before the test starts. The idea is that the tester understands how the system works so that they don't need to waste time analysing the system and putting together attacks. In the real world it is unlikely that the attacker would fully understand our system. However, if we apply the scenario that, say, a cleaner has been collecting documents to be given to an attacker then we can better appreciate the importance of this test. A white box test forms probably the most dangerous of attacks given the tester's knowledge of the system. It's much better that we conduct the most thorough assessment rather than wait for an attacker to exploit the system. The other point of a white box test is to bring the tester inside the network. Connecting them from outside the network behind a firewall only tells you how secure the firewall is, not the system itself. If we know a system is secure after a white box test then we have a high degree of assurance that a black box test would be unsuccessful.

Advantages:

- Faster, so costs less
- Thorough test.

Disadvantages:

- Not likely in a real scenario.

Black box testing

Black box testing is the opposite to white box testing, which means that the tester has no prior knowledge of the system itself. Black box testing emulates the most lifelike scenario of a hacker attacking the system. Often testers are only provided with an IP address and a timeframe within which to attack the system. Although black box testing is the most lifelike, they often don't teach us much about the system's vulnerabilities. Often the test team is a service that has been brought in and they only have a limited time to attack the system. In reality a hacker has much more time to watch, analyse the system and formulate an attack. I recommend coupling a black box test with a white box test afterwards, stipulating that anything learned during the black box test can be applied during the white box assessment.

Advantages:

- Lifelike scenario.

Disadvantages:

- Doesn't usually teach us much
- Takes a long time if we want to be thorough (costly).

Vulnerability assessments

Vulnerability assessments are a favourite of mine as they are often cheap and quick and can offer a quick security assessment of a system. They are particularly useful in an agile working environment where we want to deliver systems quickly. Vulnerability assessments can be carried out using software such as Nessus or Metasploit. These tools can be configured to log in to the target system in order to conduct their scans, and they then produce reports with recommended actions. These scans are a good assurance control before deploying software and can be configured to run on a regular basis so that you can check a system's configuration hasn't changed to make it less secure. Vulnerability scans are also useful in verifying that patches have been applied across the estate. These scanners regularly receive updates to check for the latest vulnerabilities, so including them in a patch-management process can be extremely useful, especially in ensuring a system hasn't been missed.

Something to note with vulnerability assessments is that they are automated, so the results need human analysis to confirm the results and recommendations. Also, a system may be configured with an inherent vulnerability that is part of its general running, for example a web server will always have a degree of weakness as part of its purpose. However, what we can do with our vulnerability assessment reports is use them as part of our white box testing. So pick out the vulnerabilities that concern us and ask the testers to try to exploit those weaknesses and then tell us how easy it was. We can also use these reports to see if our black box testers were able to find the vulnerabilities and exploit them. If vulnerabilities are difficult to exploit then we may choose to live with them.

Advantages:

- Cheap
- Fast
- Automated
- Can be scheduled.

Disadvantages:

- Requires human analysis
- Can only be run on common recognised software.

Build reviews

A build review is carried out on the underlying infrastructure. Operating systems are insecure out of the box, so the administrator will need to customise the system so that it can provide the service needed and also harden it from attack. Despite popular belief even Linux systems are insecure out of the box. A vulnerability assessment is a good place to start but the real advantage is human analysis of the system. An automated tool only looks at individual settings whereas a good build reviewer considers the aggregate of those settings and understands if a vulnerability is introduced through a certain combination. The build reviewer also understands the context of certain settings without blindly flagging them up as vulnerabilities. A good build review is often time consuming and expensive. However, this expense can be offset when reviewing baseline systems because the same build can be deployed multiple times. So if an organisation wants to spin up separate Linux web servers, we can test the original build and then deploy it multiple times. Of course some work should still be done to ensure no settings have changed once deployed and a regular review should be scheduled of the build to take into account new vulnerabilities and system upgrades.

Advantages:

- Thorough
- Human analysis.

Disadvantages:

- Time consuming
- Costly
- People can miss things.

Code reviews

Code reviews focus on the software your team has developed, and the task can be done securely and insecurely. For example, some types of database calls can leave SQL injection vulnerabilities whereas other types of calls can prevent this from occurring. A code review can ensure the software that has been written has not introduced these vulnerabilities and has followed best practice. Code reviews can be carried out in many ways: you can have developers conduct peer reviews, use an independent review party or use an automated tool such as Gerrit (Java) or Review Board (Python).

Peer reviews are the quickest and cheapest way of conducting a code review, as often the resource and knowledge is there ready to be used. I recommend having developers who haven't written the code review it, or if your organisation is large enough then have a separate development team. The key benefit of your own people conducting the review is that they already have some idea of the system and the code they are reviewing. This is also a double-edged sword, however, because by using internal knowledge it is likely that the same mistakes will be made across teams and not be spotted.

Third-party reviews are very useful from an independent point of view. The reviewers have no bias and have experience in reviewing lots of different code from organisations. This can be particularly beneficial for injecting new knowledge and new best practice into the organisation. The drawbacks to third-party reviews is the time and expense in bringing the reviewer up to speed with the code they are reviewing, and it can also mean that they might overlook something if they fail to understand the system.

Automated code reviews like our vulnerability assessment can be an extremely useful way of conducting a baseline assessment and ensuring a minimum level of quality and security. Another benefit is that often these tools allow you to customise and add your own review points. This can be useful if you want to review code and ensure it follows a consistent approach as well as security. Also, if we identify an insecure piece of code during a manual assessment then we can create a script to scan the rest of the codebase to ensure this problem doesn't exist elsewhere. The real advantage to creating your own scripts is re-use: once the time has been spent creating the script it can then be re-used over and over to check for that vulnerability.

Physical assessment

Physical assessments assess the security of an office or data centre. The aim is to ensure the systems can physically be accessed or stolen. An organisation will typically have a data centre(s) where multiple systems are located. I don't recommend carrying out a physical assessment every time a new system is deployed there as this becomes onerous. Instead carry out a detailed annual assessment or perhaps when adding a new sensitive system, the reason being that the level of risk posed to the data centre may change with the new system moving there.

Physical assessments come in two flavours: an inspection of the data centre or an attempted break-in where the assessor tries to gain unauthorised access. An inspection usually involves the assessor being escorted around the facility noting their findings. The other test where the assessor attempts to break in is far more sensitive and requires a lot more management on your behalf. You first need to discuss in more detail with the assessor about how they intend to attack the facility; you need to agree things such as whether can they cut a fence or break a window to gain access. Remember that these things will need fixing after the test. Also, you need to give the tester a 'get out of jail free card' in case he is arrested! You could brief the security guard of an attempted break-in in the next month so the police aren't called if the assessor is caught.

Scoping the test

We now have awareness of all the different types of testing we can do, but we need to bring that together into a penetration test. Remember that you have to secure the entire system, whereas the attacker only needs to exploit one weakness. There is no point in securing the front door and spending a lot of effort testing it only to forget about the back door. A good penetration test includes a mixture of tests and includes at least the live system. Depending on how your test systems are deployed and used, there may not be a need to include them. For example, if those test systems only have test data on them and aren't connected to the Internet, you need to assess the risks posed by the test systems and make a decision on whether they are in scope or not. Based on the previous section on documenting the system I have put together the following basic diagram showing the physical systems:

The diagram is extremely simple, and only needs to give the testers a high-level understanding of what needs to be tested. As well as the diagram the testers need a written description of what is to be tested.

Web server: IP 123.123.123.123

The web server provides the frontend for the service, and the service is deployed to an Amazon Web Service instance. The server is using Apache on Linux and has been developed using Java.

The server is subject to the following tests:

- Build review
- External penetration test.

External firewall: IP 124.124.124.124

The external firewall is a SonicWall and protects the DMZ from attack. It is configured to allow HTTPS connections through on port 443.

The server is subject to the following tests:

- Build review (firewall rules)
- External penetration test.

Reverse proxy: IP 125.125.125.125

The reverse proxy is an NginX proxy and manages the incoming connections to the network to the e-commerce server only.

The server is subject to the following tests:

- Build review
- External penetration test.

e-commerce server: IP 126.126.126.126

The e-commerce server provides the business logic and is responsible for carrying out transactions. The system has been deployed on an Ubuntu Server OS using Apache. The service itself has been created using Java.

The server is subject to the following tests:

- Code review
- Build review
- External penetration test.

Database server: IP 127.127.127.127

The database server runs on Windows Server 2008 and is an Oracle Database. The database itself stores product and user data.

The server is subject to the following tests:

- External penetration test
- Vulnerability assessment.

It is probable that the test team will have questions based on the scope. They will want to clarify whether the systems are in use for live services, and they may have questions about the technology deployed to them and will want to confirm server numbers. Many penetration testing firms will help you create a scope for a test but they will of course charge for this service. The more information you can provide, the quicker they can put together a proposal for testing your system.

Trusting the Testers

Trusting testers is important, as these people potentially have direct access to your data. You need to have trust in the assessor and trust they have the technical ability so that they are thorough and do not accidentally compromise the data. Ask if they have undergone a government security check, and consider a criminal records check as an alternative. Judging someone's technical ability is much harder; ensure the testers have experience testing real live systems like yours. You want to vary the amount of experience depending on the sensitivity of the system being tested.

Non-disclosure agreements are very common in the private sector. Often testers will, especially when carrying out white box testing, have access to sensitive information. The last thing you want to do is share company secrets with someone who will inform a rival.

You may implement an agreement with a particular firm to provide testing on a regular basis. There are advantages from a trust and ability point of view but there are also drawbacks. For example, if the same testers test your systems and they miss a vulnerability, it is likely they will miss it again. Rotate who carries out the testing to ensure a greater chance of finding vulnerabilities, and this can be done by forming an agreement with two or more testing firms.

Implementing Fixes

Of course now that you have a list of vulnerabilities you are going to want to fix them. There are two key ways of managing this depending on how important the fixes are and how quickly you want to implement them. You can either set up a live support team to fix vulnerabilities as they are found, or you can wait for the full report and then implement fixes on a risk-based approach.

Setting up a live team to work with the penetration testing team can be chaotic but also very rewarding. One of the key benefits is having the testers retest systems to confirm fixes have been implemented effectively. If lots of remediation work is needed after a penetration test then you may need a second test, and using this fix method avoids this (assuming things aren't really bad). If the systems are live with real users, many patches require a system restart, so fixing during working hours could be disruptive to the business and cause you a lot of problems without engaging the proper management people. If you are fortunate to have a change-management team who have the relevant business contacts and have experience in managing this sort of agile patching then great, otherwise I recommend not using this method.

The more traditional method is to wait for the full penetration test report. Understand the finds and put them into context. A critical vulnerability identified in the report may not be as critical, for example if a web-based vulnerability is found and the server is in the core of the network then the vulnerability is less likely to be exploited by an attacker. Conversely, a vulnerability labelled medium could be on a system connected to the Internet, which would make the system a higher risk as it's more likely to be attacked.

CHAPTER 10: INFORMATION SECURITY POLICY

Chapter Overview

This chapter introduces the topic of security policies, explaining their importance giving you a baseline from which to build a strong foundation. If you are looking to attain ISO27001 certification then you will need to produce security policies to form your information security management system (ISMS). This chapter is not intended to advise you on how to achieve this level of maturity, but give you an appreciation for why these policies exist and how they can be used to achieve your organisation's goals and objectives.

It is important that security policies are created in line with the organisation's culture; they should be an enabler, not a hindrance to staff. For example, if staff need to use laptops as part of their jobs then the policies should define their behaviour so that staff know what they can and cannot do, and so that they know how to use the laptops in a safe manner. What the policies should not do is impose so many rules that staff stop using laptops and taking advantage of mobile working. It is about striking a balance and achieving a level of protection suitable to the risks involved.

In this chapter I explain some of the advantages of good security policies, which will help you justify to the business the policies you identify a requirement for. I also describe how policies should be laid out and some of the key terms and words that should be used. I then explain how to make sure your policies are effective and are followed, or as I like to say, giving your policy teeth! Finally, I describe some of the key basic policies I believe all organisations should have.

Objectives

In this chapter you will learn the following:

- The benefits of security policies
- Key or baseline security policies
- How a policy should be presented
- Ways to ensure your policies are read
- Giving your policies teeth.

The Advantages of Security Policies

The advantages of security policies are typically very much the same as any other policy only they come with the aim of maintaining the organisation's security.

The first advantage is that the policy informs staff what is expected of them. When staff are given access to a new system or piece of equipment they should also be provided with a copy (or provided a link to an intranet page) of the policy that applies. You should seek their agreement that they understand the policy and that they will follow it. By doing so you will have confidence that the system or device will be used as expected.

When using a system or a device staff often face the same reoccurring questions and points where they need to make a decision. An example I often encounter is when our staff visit a conference and are given the slide deck on a USB pen; they often ask if they are allowed to plug this into their desktop and whether they are allowed to copy data for the device. By creating a policy and making staff aware of the policy, staff can answer many of their questions by referring to the policy.

In larger organisations it is important to ensure a consistent approach, especially when large company networks are involved. A malware infection could quickly spread from PC to PC or destroy data on shared network drives. By producing clear and concise policies we can ensure our staff follow the same standard security practices.

When new staff join the organisation it is important to bring them up to speed as quickly as possible. Often they will have become used to a previous working culture and it will take them time to adapt. By documenting the security policies not only can you bring them up to speed quickly but they also have a point of reference to make sure they are following your practices.

The final advantage is one of liability, not just for the company but also for staff. If a member of staff consistently fails to follow the rules set out in a policy, this can be used for grounds for disciplinary action. If the policies are not documented, you will find it extremely difficult to ensure a consistent way of working is being followed by all staff. Conversely, if a member of staff follows the rules set out in a policy and there is a security breach then they can defend their actions by showing that they followed the policy. A member of staff cannot be reasonably punished if they followed the rules set.

Identifying What Policies You Need

Later in this chapter I describe some of the more common security policies that you'll come across and will possibly need depending on your business. However, just because it seems like a good idea or because someone else has one doesn't mean you should have the same policy. Like all security controls policies and their content, they should only be created where there is a business need for one.

Security policies should be created after carrying out a risk assessment. For example, if our business decides that all employees should have laptops then we should carry out a risk assessment looking at the risks of staff having laptops. This risk assessment will help us decide the security controls needed, which will then help form the security policy for using a laptop.

How a Policy Should be Written

When writing policies it is important to keep them to the point and ensure your instructions are clear and easy to understand. Note that a policy describes what must be done but typically not how it should be done; that level of detail would exist in a security operating procedure. I recommend using the following key terms: Must, Should and Will not. This is similar to the MoSCoW method that adds the additional term of Could.

Must describes something that must be done. For example, staff must wear their ID passes at all times.

Should describes something that is highly desirable. For example, when using a laptop in a company place you should be aware of anyone trying to shoulder surf.

Won't describes something that must not be done, which can be written as 'will not' if it makes for better reading. An example could be staff will not leave laptops unattended in public places.

Giving Your Policies Teeth

It doesn't matter how reasonable or pragmatic your policies

are, there will be those people who will not follow the rules laid out in them. Either they see the rules as excessive or don't fully understand the risks (or don't take the time to understand them). Luckily these instances are few and far between, but you must ensure your policy is obeyed. This is best achieved by there being some sort of disciplinary action taken should a policy not be followed. This is often referred to as a policy breach.

You will probably find that it is not within your power to define what disciplinary action should be carried out if a policy is breached. However, by now you should have built a good relationship with management (*Chapter 1*) and they would have been involved with the risk assessment. Because of this they will have helped you define the impact on the business should the policy rules be breached. What this means is that they have some appetite in ensuring the policy is enforced and to what level that enforcement is carried out. Some suggestions for ensuring compliance with the policy are as follows:

- Employee is given a reminder of the policy rules, which can be done verbally but I recommend following this up in writing (email) and possibly copying their line manager. This will ensure you have a record if continued non-compliance continues.

- Withdrawal of company privileges: this could be the withdrawn use of a company car park or maybe an iPad. The point being made is that the staff member can no longer be trusted to use the asset securely, therefore they can no longer use it at all.

- Formal warning: the employee is formally warned, which needs to be done in line with human resources and any formal policy they have for managing this process.

- Finally, and this really should be a last resort and reserved for only the most severe breaches, termination of contract.

To successfully implement these penalties you need management approval and possibly the board and human resources to agree.

Key Security Policies

The next section seems contradictory based on my previous statement about policies coming from risk assessments and that you shouldn't just copy what someone else is doing. However, I want to describe the more common policies and mention the key elements that they maintain. Think of this as more of a starting point to be considered rather than a foundation for the creation policies.

Remember that good policies are created based on risk management: if there are no risks then you don't need to create a policy.

IT Usage

The IT usage policy (or computer usage) is the keystone of all computer-related policies. It sets the foundation for the other policies that you may decide to implement and shapes the way your organisation works with IT. Some key points that this policy may include are:

- PC locked when unattended
- Complex password used and not written down
- Rules on plugging in USB devices
- Rules on plugging devices into the network

- Do not share account credentials.

Email Usage

The email usage policy is another key policy if your staff have access to email. Email is a useful tool in business and can help people to collaborate, so it is important that any policy isn't too prohibitive. Some key points are:

- Can email be used for personal use?
- Is the use of personal email allowed during lunch times?
- What can be sent or discussed in email and what can't?
- Do emails require a protective marking in the subject line?

Internet Usage

Much the same as email, the Internet is an extremely useful asset to any business. Responsible use of the Internet should be encouraged. As such the policy should be written in much the same way. Staff should know what the conditions of use are so that they can feel confident they aren't breaking policy. Some policy rules that you may want to consider include:

- What websites are prohibited?
- Can the Internet be used for personal use?
- Is Internet use monitored?
- Can files be downloaded from the Internet? What about executables?

Laptop Usage

Laptops are becoming the preferred platform for staff, slowly replacing desktop PCs. They are now offering similar performance but with much more flexibility in terms of location, and it is this flexibility that poses the most risk. Most work office environments are secure but a laptop can be used anywhere – a pub or a train for example. The size of a laptop makes it very easy to steal or its public use could allow someone else to read the screen. Some policy points to consider are:

- Where can the laptop be used?
- Does it need to be secured physically?
- Where should it be stored when not in use?
- What do you need to do if it's lost or stolen?

Ways of Ensuring Your Policy is Read

Having your policy read can often be very challenging. A very descriptive and well-written document can become very long and put people off reading it, or even worse force them to skim-read it and miss important points.

Two common ways of encouraging a policy to be read are to have a reward, for example a prize draw, or a quiz that offers a prize for those who answer the most questions. The problem with these is that policies are constantly changing and evolving to meet business needs, so having a quiz and a prize are impractical. Additionally, people will read the policy only to win a prize rather than seeing the value of the policy and following its instruction. Some better ways include the following:

Allow people to be actively involved in the review and creation of the policy. Getting user feedback on what works and what rules are impractical will help you fine-tune the policy. People will be better engaged and more likely to follow the rules that they shape.

Produce a 60-second guide. Make a very succinct set of policy rules with reasoning or explanation removed. This will be useful to those who want a refresher or are in a hurry. If people know they can read the entire policy quickly then they are more likely to read it cover to cover. If they don't understand some of the rules or wish to challenge them then the full policy can then be referred to for clarification.

Questions and answers. When you publish a policy you will encounter lots of questions from staff members, and often these questions are the same. You may find it useful to hold questions and answers meetings and allow people to personally ask questions about the rules. These sessions can then be documented and shared with people who need to follow the policy. They allow people to engage better with the policy and further understand it, which in turn motivates them to read the policy document.

ITG RESOURCES

IT Governance Ltd sources, creates and delivers products and services to meet the real-world, evolving IT governance needs of today's organisations, directors, managers and practitioners.

The ITG website (*www.itgovernance.co.uk*) is the international one-stop-shop for corporate and IT governance information, advice, guidance, books, tools, training and consultancy. On the website you will find the following pages related to the subject matter of this book:

www.itgovernance.co.uk/infosec.aspx

www.itgovernance.co.uk/iso27001.aspx.

Publishing Services

IT Governance Publishing (ITGP) is the world's leading IT-GRC publishing imprint that is wholly owned by IT Governance Ltd.

With books and tools covering all IT governance, risk and compliance frameworks, we are the publisher of choice for authors and distributors alike, producing unique and practical publications of the highest quality, in the latest formats available, which readers will find invaluable.

www.itgovernancepublishing.co.uk is the website dedicated to ITGP. Other titles published by ITGP that may be of interest include:

- Once more unto the Breach

    www.itgovernance.co.uk/shop/p-985.aspx

- The Case for ISO27001:2013

  www.itgovernance.co.uk/shop/p-1667-the-case-for-iso-27001-2013-second-edition.aspx

- Nine Steps to Success: An ISO27001:2013 Implementation Overview

  www.itgovernance.co.uk/shop/p-963-nine-steps-to-success-an-iso-270012013-implementation-overview-second-edition.aspx.

We also offer a range of off-the-shelf toolkits that give comprehensive, customisable documents to help users create the specific documentation they need to properly implement a management system or standard. Written by experienced practitioners and based on the latest best practice, ITGP toolkits can save months of work for organisations working towards compliance with a given standard.

To see the full range of toolkits available please visit:

www.itgovernance.co.uk/shop/c-129-toolkits.aspx.

Books and tools published by IT Governance Publishing (ITGP) are available from all business booksellers and the following websites:

www.itgovernance.eu   *www.itgovernanceusa.com*

www.itgovernance.in   *www.itgovernancesa.co.za*

www.itgovernance.asia.

Training Services

Staff training is an essential component of the information security triad of people, processes and technology, and of building an enterprise-wide security culture. IT Governance's ISO 27001 Learning Pathway provides information security courses from Foundation to Advanced level, with qualifications awarded by IBITGQ.

Many courses are available in Live Online as well as classroom formats, so delegates can learn and achieve essential career progression from the comfort of their own homes and offices.

Delegates passing the exams associated with our ISO 27001 Learning Pathway will gain qualifications from IBITGQ, including CIS F, CIS IA, CIS LI, CIS LA, CIS RM and CIS 2013 UP.

IT Governance is an acknowledged leader in the world of ISO27001 and information security management training. Our practical, hands-on approach is delivered by experienced practitioners, who focus on improving your knowledge, developing your skills, and awarding relevant, industry-recognised certifications. Our fully integrated and structured learning paths accommodate delegates with various levels of knowledge, and our courses can be delivered in a variety of formats to suit all delegates.

For more information about IT Governance's ISO 27001 Learning Pathway, please see: *www.itgovernance.co.uk/iso27001-information-security-training.aspx.*

For information on any of our many other courses, including PCI DSS compliance, business continuity, IT governance, service management and professional certification courses, please see: *www.itgovernance.co.uk/training.aspx*.

Professional Services and Consultancy

ISO 27001, the international standard for information security management, sets out the requirements of an information security management system (ISMS), a holistic approach to information security that encompasses people, processes, and technology. Only by using this approach to information security can organisations hope to instil an enterprise-wide security culture.

Implementing, maintaining and continually improving an ISMS can, however, be a daunting task. Fortunately, IT Governance's consultants offer a comprehensive range of flexible, practical support packages to help organisations of any size, sector or location to implement an ISMS and achieve certification to ISO 27001.

We have already helped more than 150 organisations to implement an ISMS, and with project support provided by our consultants, you can implement ISO 27001 in your organisation.

At IT Governance we understand that information security is a business issue, not just an IT one. Our consultancy services assist organisations in properly managing their information technology strategies and achieving strategic goals.

For more information on our ISO 27001 consultancy service, please see: *www.itgovernance.co.uk/iso27001_consultancy.aspx.*

For general information about our other consultancy services, including for ISO20000, ISO22301, Cyber Essentials, the PCI DSS, Data Protection and more, please see: *www.itgovernance.co.uk/consulting.aspx.*

Newsletter

IT governance is one of the hottest topics in business today, not least because it is also the fastest moving.

You can stay up to date with the latest developments across the whole spectrum of IT governance subject matter, including; risk management, information security, ITIL and IT service management, project governance, compliance and so much more, by subscribing to ITG's core publications and topic alert emails.

Simply visit our subscription centre and select your preferences:

www.itgovernance.co.uk/newsletter.aspx.

EU for product safety is Stephen Evans, The Mill Enterprise Hub, Stagreenan, Drogheda, Co. Louth, A92 CD3D, Ireland. (servicecentre@itgovernance.eu)

www.ingramcontent.com/pod-product-compliance
Lightning Source LLC
Chambersburg PA
CBHW070835070326
40690CB00009B/1559